THE QUIET MAN

Ireland Into Film

Series editors:
Keith Hopper (text) and Gráinne Humphreys (images)

Ireland Into Film is the first project in a number of planned collaborations between Cork University Press and the Film Institute of Ireland. The general aim of this publishing initiative is to increase the critical understanding of 'Irish' Film (i.e. films made in, or about, Ireland). This particular series brings together writers and scholars from the fields of Film and Literary Studies to examine notable adaptations of Irish literary texts.

Other titles available in this series:

The Dead (Kevin Barry)
December Bride (Lance Pettitt)
This Other Eden (Fidelma Farley)
The Informer (Patrick F. Sheeran)
The Field (Cheryl Temple Herr)

Forthcoming titles:

Nora (Gerardine Meaney)
The Butcher Boy (Colin MacCabe)
Dancing at Lughnasa (Joan Dean)

Ireland Into Film

THE QUIET MAN

Luke Gibbons

CORK UNIVERSITY PRESS

in association with
THE FILM INSTITUTE OF IRELAND

First published in 2002 by
Cork University Press
Cork
Ireland

British Library Cataloguing in Publication Data
A CIP catalogue record for this book is available from the British Library.

ISBN 1 85918 287 9

Typesetting by Red Barn Publishing, Skeagh, Skibbereen

Printed by ColourBooks Ltd, Baldoyle, Dublin

Ireland Into Film receives financial assistance from
the Arts Council / An Chomhairle Ealaíon and the Film Institute of Ireland

For Louis and Betty Maguire,
and in memory of Bernadette (Ben) Coyle

CONTENTS

LIST OF ILLUSTRATIONS

The four page insert contains photographs taken on set by Bill Maguire and is reproduced courtesy of the author.

Acknowledgements

Toilers in the elysian fields of Innisfree can only be grateful to Des MacHale, whose *The Complete Guide to* The Quiet Man is the work of a true enthusiast, and whose eye for detail gives even Joyceans a run for their money. Future scholars will also owe a considerable debt to Joseph McBride's massive biography of Ford – the prose equivalent, perhaps, of the director's beloved Monument Valley. Tag Gallagher's detailed study of Ford's work, film by film, set new standards for research on the director, and I hope this short book lives up to them. My editors, Keith Hopper and Gráinne Humphreys, persuaded me in the first place to re-visit ideas I had first sketched many years ago in *Cinema and Ireland* (co-authored with Kevin Rockett and John Hill), and I am grateful for their patience and professionalism throughout. I also wish to thank Emma Keogh and Eugene Finn, both of whom gave me invaluable help with archival material in the Library of the Film Institute of Ireland, and the Irish Film Archive. The creative flair and expertise of three people have made a distinctive contribution to the book: Bernard O'Donoghue, Oxford University, for his wonderful poem on 'The Quiet Man', which acts as the epigraph; Stephanie Rains, Dublin City University, for her pioneering work on Irish travelogue films and Irish-American cultural perceptions; and Caoilfhionn Ní Bheacháin, University of Limerick, for her assiduous research on John Ford's visit to Ireland during the Truce in 1921.

As a teacher, I am greatly indebted to all those students and colleagues at Dublin City University, The Tisch School of Arts at New York University and, in recent years, at the University of Notre Dame, who have put up with my exposition of many of the arguments developed in this book – though students, at times, may have felt they were witnessing live impersonations of scenes from the film rather than a lecture. Dudley Andrew, Des Bell, Jeff Chown, Farrel Corcoran, John Hill, Martin McLoone, Stephanie McBride,

Meaghan Morris, Diane Negra, Stephen Rea, Kevin Rockett and Paul Willemen have shaped my ideas on cinema over many years, and, more recently, friends and former students, among them Marion Casey, Maeve Connolly, Rachael Dowling, Debbie Ging, Katherine Mullin, Lance Pettitt, Stephanie Rains, Orla Ryan and Jessica Scarlata, have brought a whole range of new perspectives to bear on my understanding of Irish/American cinema and contemporary Irish culture. If I single out the late Aine O'Connor for special mention, those who knew and cherished her will understand why.

Closer to home, Dolores, Laura and Barry have helped to make my own White O'Morn, even if I have made a poor Quiet Man. I owe a special debt to Dolores's uncle-in-law Louis (Bill) Maguire, who presented me with his own heirloom of the film, an album of snapshots taken while acting as John Wayne's double. This book is dedicated to him, his wife Betty and her sister, the late Bernadette Coyle.

The editors would also like to thank Sheila Pratschke, Lar Joye, Michael Davitt, Luke Dodd, Dennis Kennedy, Kevin Rockett, Ellen Hazelkorn, Seán Ryder, Gearóid Ó Tuathaigh, Cormac Ó Comhraí, Thomas Byrne, St Cross College (Oxford), the School of Irish Studies Foundation and the Arts Council of Ireland.

Special thanks to Ben Cloney, Lee Murphy, Emma Keogh and the staff of the Irish Film Archive, Lady Killanin, Paddy Rock, Gerry Collins, Viacom Consumer Products, Universal Pictures, Cló Iar Chonnachta, Gerard Farrelly, National Library, Belenof Publications, Merlin Films, Kenny's Bookshop and Agence Photographic de la Réunion des Musées Nationaux.

All images may be sourced at the Irish Film Centre Archive.

The Quiet Man

One of the great films, by general consent,
It could have been called 'The Quiet American',
Or, for that matter, 'The Violent Irishman':
Trim John Wayne, not easily roused, but once roused
His vengeance a wonder of the western world,
With Maureen O'Hara, for all her wish
For independence, kicking impotently
On his shoulder. We saw it in Manchester,
On holiday from the hayfields of North Cork,
During the Korean War, at a time when films
Ran continuously. We came in, aptly enough,
At the culminating meadow fight,
Stayed for Tom and Jerry and the Pathé News,
Before leaving at the point we'd started at,
With McLaglen lying battered in the hay.

Bernard O'Donoghue

John Ford, as the son of immigrants, found himself culturally suspended between Ireland's potato famine and the American Dream.
Charles Ramirez Berg, 'The Margin as Centre: the Multicultural Dynamics of John Ford's Westerns', 2001[1]

In a memorable scene in *E.T.* (dir. Steven Spielberg, 1982), the housebound alien takes to the drink while his host, Elliot (Henry Thomas), is at school and, between hiccups, improvises a remote control to change channels on the television blaring in the background. Suddenly, *The Quiet Man* (1952) appears on the screen and as E.T. gazes in wonder at Sean Thornton's (John Wayne) return to his windswept cottage in Innisfree he is overcome by nostalgia for his own home and the world he has lost. E.T. is not the only one thinking this way, for his longings are transferred by telepathy to Elliot at school who is about to chloroform a frog imprisoned in a jar in biology class. Elliot is instantly seized by a desire to return the frogs to their home in the woods, and no sooner has Sean Thornton pulled Mary Kate Danaher (Maureen O'Hara) back into the cottage on the television screen in front of E.T. than Elliot finds himself re-enacting the same scene with a bewildered schoolgirl, dressed in a blue top and red skirt like Mary Kate in the film. As *The Quiet Man* theme song, 'The Isle of Innisfree', washes over the soundtrack, it all proves too much for the inebriated alien and, demonstrating that more than one Irish stereotype has gone to his head, he passes out, dreaming of his Innisfree among the stars.[2]

The rear-view mirror of nostalgia is always tinted by desire but in *E.T.* this is more the case than usual. In Ford's film, Mary Kate is wearing a blue top but in Spielberg's version it is green, as is her

Plate 1. E.T. watches The Quiet Man *on television.*

traditional shawl. This green, offset by her white apron and flaming gold hair, was also superimposed on the posters and publicity stills for *The Quiet Man*, signalling its evocation of national character and 'mother Ireland' as much as that of the individual stars or characters. That Spielberg is not the only modern director to see green where none was intended in *The Quiet Man* is clear from the homage paid to a darker side of Ford's troubled comedy in one of the other great films of the 1980s, Martin Scorsese's *Raging Bull* (1980). For Scorsese, the traumatic flashback sequence of a death in the ring – which interrupts the goodwill and bonhomie of Sean and Mary Kate's marriage ceremony – is the true precursor of the murderous fury unleashed in *Raging Bull*, the garish colours highlighting its nightmarish qualities:

> The one use of colour in a fight sequence that really impressed me was the flashback in Ford's *The Quiet Man*,

when Wayne looks down and realizes he's killed his
opponent, and I'll never forget the vibrance of his emerald
green trunks.[3]

There is green (not exactly vibrant) in the sequence, but it does not
belong to Sean Thornton's trunks, which are dark red; rather, it is
discernible in his professional boxing name – 'Trooper Thorn' – and
his lucky mascot, a four-leafed shamrock, emblazoned on the back of
his second's shirt. But Scorsese is correct to point to a disturbing
undercurrent of death and violence which pierces the surface levity
of *The Quiet Man*, and in *Raging Bull* it is as if Sean Thornton's
horrific flashback, which barely lasts a minute, is stretched to full epic
feature length.

Not least of the paradoxes of *The Quiet Man*'s undisputed status as
the emblematic representation of the Irish on the screen is that while
it has garnered accolades from directors as diverse as Spielberg and
Scorsese, for others it is the bane of Irish cinema. If, as William Blake
once claimed of Sir Joshua Reynolds, 'this man was hired to depress
art', then *The Quiet Man* was seen by successive waves of Irish
filmmakers and critics as setting back Irish cinema for decades. But if
Ford's romantic comedy found little favour with those engaged in
developing an indigenous Irish film industry, it has never lost its
touch with popular audiences. From the outset, it proved to be
Republic studio's most successful film, winning two Oscars – Ford for
'Best Director', Winton C. Hoch and Archie Stout for 'Best Colour
Cinematography' – and receiving seven Oscar nominations.[4] In the
distinguished company of Fred Zinnemann's *High Noon*, it lost out as
best film to Cecil B. De Mille's *The Greatest Show on Earth*, but won
the International Prize at the Venice Film Festival (1952) and the
Outstanding Annual Direction Award from the Directors' Guild
(1953). Its worldwide success coincided with the establishment of
Bord Fáilte, the Irish Tourist Board, in July 1952,[5] and, as we shall
see, it acted as a blueprint for subsequent travelogue films promoting

Ireland as a tourist attraction. Just as the new Irish Film Board was making its presence felt in the 1980s, *The Quiet Man* came back to haunt Irish cinema, appearing on video in 1985 and selling almost 200,000 copies in the first four years in Britain alone.[6] It features regularly in website polls for the 'Best Movies' or 'Top 100' films, being advertised as '#44 Favorite Flick' of all time on one site, along with Ashley Shannon's *Irish Blessings: a Photographic Celebration* ('A collection of everything that is right about Ireland, with images of countryside, towns and houses. . .').[7] In a 1996 Centenary of Cinema poll, it was voted by *Irish Times* readers as the best Irish film, and its cult-like status has increased in recent years with the development of a cottage industry, so to speak, around the locations and sites of the production in Cong, County Mayo. The opening of the Quiet Man Heritage Centre in 1996 has given rise to a run in *The Quiet Man* souvenirs and memorabilia, and for the true aficionado there is the Quiet Man quiz-book, with questions such as 'Who was the caretaker of the graveyard at the time of the author's [i.e. Maurice Walsh] burial?' and 'Who owns the Quiet Man restaurant in Cong?' (Answer: 'Mrs Gibbons').

Ford had been captivated by Maurice Walsh's original story 'The Quiet Man' on its first publication in the *Saturday Evening Post* in 1933 (see Chapter 1), but despite repeated attempts, first in 1937 and then throughout the 1940s, was unable to see it through into production. Following her debut with Ford as Angharad Morgan in *How Green Was My Valley* (1941), Maureen O'Hara was cast as early as 1944 to play the female lead, and though there were suggestions that Robert Ryan, a former boxer, would make a suitable male lead,[8] John Wayne was the natural choice after his pairing with O'Hara in Ford's *Rio Grande* (1950). Barry Fitzgerald and Victor McLaglen were also waiting on call with 'handshake contracts' (as Maureen O'Hara described them), but some of the more engaging cameos were provided by actors who were last-minute additions to the cast, such as Jack MacGowran (who substituted for Noel Purcell). Ford's resolve

Plate 2.   The Quiet Man cottage museum.

to bring *The Quiet Man* to the screen finally paid off in 1950 when
Argosy, the production company he formed with Merian C. Cooper,
signed a three-film contract with Republic, a largely B-movie studio
run by the cantankerous Herbert J. Yates which had the advantage of
having John Wayne on its books. The deal was that if Ford turned a

Plate 3. The Quiet Man quiz book.

western around first, with many of the ensemble already cast for *The Quiet Man*, Republic would then fund Ford's cherished Irish project. Ford took no risks with the first film, shooting *Rio Grande* with John Wayne and Maureen O'Hara, and, when this sweetener proved successful, Yates gave the go-ahead for shooting on an expensive overseas location – a first for Republic. To further ensure the film would finally make it into production, Wayne and O'Hara agreed to take cuts in their fees – Wayne accepting $100,000 and O'Hara $65,000.[9]

Ford began filming in Cong early in June 1951, using Ashford Castle as his base of operations. The shoot lasted for six weeks, itself becoming part of local folklore. The involvement of local people – Joe Milotte as John Wayne's stand-in, Bill Maguire as his double; Mary Maguire as Maureen O'Hara's stand-in, Etta Vaughan as her double; local boxer Martin Thornton as Victor McLaglen's double – plus continuous coverage of the shoot in the local newspapers imparted a festive atmosphere and sense of community to the set not unlike its imaginary counterpart in the film. As with some of the most inspired casting decisions, Cong was not Ford's original choice of location, his preference being for Spiddal, the village from which both his father and mother had emigrated in 1872. As Ford wrote to his friend Lord Killanin in 1946, when Spiddal was still the intended location:

> I think we could have a lot of fun on *The Quiet Man*. It's a lovely story and I think we should go all over Ireland and get a bit of scenery here and a bit of scenery there and really make the thing a beautiful travelogue beside a really charming story.[10]

From this it is clear that Ford was not only seeking a family connection but intended to use the film as a showcase for Irish tourism from the outset. When the location shifted to Mayo, following a vacation spent in Ireland with the Killanins in 1950, Ford was still keen to pursue family ties, claiming that the parish of Dunfeeney near Cong was the original home 'from which the Feeneys were driven in days gone by' – Feeney being Ford's original family name.[11] The residues of nationalist popular memory also influenced Ford's choice of the Mayo/Galway border region for, as he put it in an interview, 'The customs shown in *The Quiet Man* are true and prevail in Connemara, which is the poorest county [*sic*] in Ireland and the only one Cromwell never conquered.' It is with this statement in mind that Tag Gallagher explains the appeal of this region for Ford: 'Connemara is a Third-

World culture, fundamentally Gaelic-Irish, but with the Roman Church and England superimposed upon the palimpsest.'[12] The irony is that in order to celebrate this sanctuary of tradition on the screen, Cong had to be modernized and brought up to speed with Hollywood production requirements. The village was prioritized for rural electrification, Ford ensuring that the cast and crew turned out for the switch-on ceremony, and the telephone system also had to be upgraded to a 24-hour service to facilitate communication with the United States.[13]

Ford's pride in his Feeney background arose from his birth as John Martin Feeney at Portland, Maine, in 1894, where his parents, both Irish speakers, had settled soon after their arrival in the United States. Ford's attachment to his ancestry extended to the Irish language, which he used to speak to Maureen O'Hara on the set of *The Quiet Man*, integrating it into the action of the film in the scene where Mary Kate confesses her marital problems to Father Lonergan (Ward Bond). Ford's determination to lay claim to his Irishness pervades not only his obvious Irish theme films but also his westerns and other classics such as *How Green Was My Valley* and *The Grapes of Wrath* (1940). Though set during the worst years of the Depression in America, *The Grapes of Wrath* reminded Ford of the harsh social conditions of nineteenth-century Ireland from which his parents had fled:

> The story was similar to the famine in Ireland, when they threw the people off the land and left them wandering on the roads to starve. That may have something to do with it – part of my Irish tradition – but I liked the idea of this family going out and trying to find their way in the world.[14]

As we shall see, similar displacements between Ireland and America occur in *The Quiet Man*: the shadow of a grim execution during the Irish War of Independence that hangs over Maurice Walsh's original book is transposed to an American setting, assuming the form of a death in the ring brought about by Sean Thornton's lust for profit –

Plate 4. 'The Isle of Innisfree'.

and blood. In *The Grapes of Wrath*, the search for a Garden of Eden out west that drives the Joad family is less an escapist fantasy than a vision of hope, a dream of the future, however utopian, that prevents the beleaguered family from succumbing to their fate in the grim days of the Depression. In a similar fashion, the pastoral vision of Ireland evoked in *The Quiet Man*, though obviously trading on tourist and emigrant fantasies of a golden age in the past, is also a way of coming to terms with trauma, loss and the experience of profound social change in Ireland.

Forty Shades of Pastoral

The Quiet Man's euphoric blend of comedy and romance belongs to the pastoral genre, an idealization of rural life that dates back to Greek literature but which received its most powerful expression in Virgil's *Eclogues*. As literary scholars have recently argued, the revival of the pastoral genre in the eighteenth century, with its notion of a 'rural retreat' and the recreation of a primitive lifestyle, was itself a product of the very modernity from which it sought to escape. As modernization – in the form of the Enclosure Acts, market relations and agricultural 'improvement' – took hold of the English countryside, it was not surprising that, in a mixture of protest and nostalgia, writers should look back to the pastoral to evoke an idealized world before 'the Fall'.[15] The pastoral was essentially an imaginary return to the second stage of society outlined in eighteenth-century theories of progress and civilization – the herding or 'shepherd' stage, before the invention of money, technology and property. The absence of money and property maintained a sense of community, the absence of technology and work (i.e. cultivation of the soil) a fusion or communion with nature.

Variations on these themes recur in *The Quiet Man*, most notably the resplendent vision of Mary Kate herding sheep in a pastoral landscape (in actual life, the manicured lawns of Ashford Castle) which first entrances Sean at the beginning of the film. Allied to this are other components of the pastoral: a strong sense of community, cutting across religious/class divisions and extending even to the collective violence of the 'Donnybrook' (a mass brawl); the emphasis on leisure and recreation (as in the racing sequence); the camaraderie of singing and humour; and the endless consumption of alcohol (the call to the bar being such that even Michaeleen Oge Flynn's (Barry Fitzgerald) horse stops, Pavlovian fashion, outside Cohan's pub). A

Plate 5. Dublin Opinion, *1952.*

profound distrust of money (the invention of money, according to the political philosopher John Locke, signalled the end of the Golden Age) also figures prominently in the story, as does an aversion to technology and work. The closest Sean Thornton approaches to manual labour is when he plants roses in front of his cottage, but even this is for sentimental reasons – in memory of his mother – which draws fire from Mary Kate: 'Fine farmer you are! Not a turnip or a cabbage or a potato around the place.' But when Sean proposes to follow up on her suggestion, she turns out to be the romantic:

> MARY KATE: Well, let's see now, we'll need a plough and a cultivator and a seed for planting and about that horse for the ploughing, we could sell that black hunter of yours.
> SEAN: I'll buy another horse for the ploughing . . . or why not a tractor?
> MARY KATE: Oh! A tractor? Nasty smelly things, and besides they're an awful price. With a horse you get other advantages. . .
> SEAN: Yeah, for the roses. . .

Though it would be easy to dismiss *The Quiet Man* as the cinematic equivalent of de Valera's 'comely maidens' speech of 1943, on account of its evasions of the harsh realities of life in the countryside, this would be equivalent to berating the fantasy sequences in *The Wizard of Oz* (dir. Victor Fleming, 1939) because they ignored the Depression in Kansas in the 1930s. (It may be, as we shall see, that *The Quiet Man* shares with *The Wizard of Oz* an association of rich Technicolor with fantasy, and that its romantic evocation of Ireland is not meant to be taken for real, any more than its beguiling surface tranquillity.) As John Barrell has argued in relation to eighteenth-century pastoral and counter-pastoral, calls for greater realism as an antidote to fantasy or romance are often 'based on the assumption that the more actualized an image, the more humane it will be'.[16] From this it is clear that realism may have as much to do with *pre*scription as with description, but it is not always clear that the morality it endorses is more humane. In much social realism, for example, depictions of the dignity of labour and the steadfastness of the 'humbler classes' are often difficult to distinguish from endorsements of the hard-work ethic and notions of the industrious, dutiful poor. Work, even if the profits go to someone else, is portrayed as ennobling, just as, conversely, in depictions of poverty, the undeserving poor are shown as bringing upon themselves their own just desserts through their feckless and improvidential ways. As against this moralistic realism, Barrell looks to one of the most powerful exercises in eighteenth-century pastoral, Oliver Goldsmith's 'The Deserted Village' (1770) – itself, perhaps, a painful idealization of an earlier vanished Ireland – for a form of radical nostalgia which challenges the sober industriousness of the work ethic.[17] Goldsmith's offence, in the eyes of his critics, was not his evocation of a carefree and leisured existence, for this was already the prerogative of the upper classes, but the implication that the lower orders had as much right to this charmed life as their superiors:

> Goldsmith disengaged the labourer from his 'proper' and 'natural' identity as a labourer, as a man born to toil, and suggested that he could be as free to dispose of his time as other poets agreed only the rich man or the shepherd was free to do. . . the charge [brought] against him is not simply that he is nostalgic for a Golden Age that never existed, but that his nostalgia is touched by a delusive and levelling radicalism.[18]

It is difficult not to suspect that the procession of rambunctious and feckless Celts through Ford's films, Irish and otherwise, was meant to cock a snoot at WASP or 'lace-curtain Irish' ideas of respectability, thrift and propriety in the United States, much as Goldsmith's pastoral questioned puritan conceptions of progress. 'America . . . Pro-hib-ition,' exclaims Michaeleen Oge Flynn with a shudder when he brings Sean Thornton from the station early in *The Quiet Man*. As Joseph McBride notes, Portland, Maine, where Ford grew up, was a 'hidebound bastion of WASP history and culture', and such notions of civility and upward mobility that existed required a disavowal of one's uncouth ethnic past.[19] Ford's insistence on placing his Irish characters, rough edges intact, in his westerns as foils to the probity of a Henry Fonda or a John Wayne can be seen as glosses on the process of assimilation itself into the larger narratives of the nation (which were not too far removed, indeed, from those of the western). Undoubtedly such narrative integration can hardly be considered successful if the ethnic underdog is restricted to providing comic asides to the march of progress – confirming rather than contesting dominant stereotypes of the Irish, Mexicans or Native Americans. However, as Ford's westerns evolve from the 1920s to the 1960s, these ethnic asides themselves mutate into disruptions or counterpoints to the main action – often slowing it down through almost sacramental notions of ritual involving eating or drinking, ceremonies of birth, marriage or death, or other expressions of family and community.[20] At times, Ford's westerns seem to aspire to the condition of musicals as set pieces featuring singing or dancing, not to mention the bar-room ballets of fist-fights or brawling, punctuate the action. These scenes of collective spectacle – receiving their most eloquent expression in the choreographed motion of the crowd going to work or bringing the body of the dead miner through the streets in *How Green Was My Valley* – cut across the individualism of the western, and its celebration of empty, lonely spaces.

In another sense, Ford's westerns may be seen as rural gangster movies in which immigrant minorities – of the kind that were later cooped up in the mean city streets of conventional gangster films – go west in pursuit of their own share in the American dream, but bringing all their cultural baggage with them. Correctly acknowledging that 'scenes of ethnic exuberance mark the major fault line between Ford's supporters and his detractors', Charles Ramirez Berg argues that 'these actions are an oppositional carnival of ethnicity meant to disrupt Mainstream [WASP] sensibilities' rooted, in Ford's eyes, in rigidity, intolerance and hypocrisy. Ford's westerns are thus replaying a clash that emigrants of his parents' generation and background had already brought with them to America, between the relatively uninhibited, vernacular culture of pre-Famine Ireland and the more rigorous, ascetic Catholicism ushered in by the Devotional Revolution in the mid nineteenth century. Almost every criticism levelled at Ford's Irish characters – communal brawling, excessive drunkenness, garrulousness, singing and dancing, aversion to discipline and the law, irreverence towards death – was the stock-in-trade of civil reformers in Ireland, whether of the nationalist or imperial stamp, as they sought to integrate the refractory culture of the lower orders into their own narratives of the nation. Much of the animus against the stage-Irishry of Boucicault's (and others) melodramas, vaudeville and the music-hall lay in the embarrassment of the newly arrived respectable classes at their barely disguised recent cultural origins.

In Ford's westerns, emigrants face the task of assimilation, but in *The Quiet Man* it is the American – or returned Irish-American – who has to undergo the rites of initiation into an unfamiliar culture. If, as Lord Killanin stated, *The Quiet Man* is 'a western made in Ireland',[21] then it is a western with an unusual ethnographic sensibility, one in which the John Wayne character can only survive by negotiating precisely the kind of cultural traditions emigrants were encouraged to jettison on their errand into the wilderness in America. *The Quiet Man* thus plays a pivotal role in the process described by Charles Ramirez Berg whereby Ford's reclaiming of his Irishness was not just an expression of an introverted ethnicity but an opening up of narrative spaces 'for a host of socially (and geographically) marginalized Others, among them various tribes of Native Americans, Mexicans and Mexican-Americans, women and African-Americans, Slavs and Poles,

Frenchmen and Italians, Swedes and Germans, poor whites and Southerners'.[22] Instead of narrowing cultural vistas, as the assimilationist ideology of the melting-pot would have it, the appropriation of modernity in the name of one's own culture led to new forms of diversity and tolerance that extended beyond the expansionist designs of the frontier ethic. Ford was at pains to emphasize that this did not mean a rejection of the modern world, or ideals of progress and change: in his moral universe, these ideals were expanded to give full scope to the diversity of the immigrant or the native Other. As he expressed it himself:

> More than having received Oscars, what counts for me is having been made a blood brother of various Indian nations. Perhaps it is my Irish atavism, my sense of reality, of the beauty of clans, in contrast to the modern world, the masses, the collective irresponsibility. Who better than an Irishman could understand the Indians, while still being stirred by the tales of the US cavalry? *We were on both sides of the epic.*[23]

As the underlying pathology and racism of *The Searchers* (1956) shows, by the mid 1950s Ford was willing to turn his camera on the dark side of the American dream, but in *The Quiet Man* America – and John Wayne's star persona – had already become tainted with mercenary profit, blood lust and death. Just as Goldsmith's 'The Deserted Village', for all its pastoral charms, is stalked by the spectre of famine ('the country blooms – a garden, and a grave'), likewise John Wayne's/Sean Thornton's 'Quiet Man', as Martin Scorsese noted, walks in the shadow of death. It is difficult to think of any romantic comedy which moves so rapidly from sunshine to thunderstorms, personal love to communal violence, comedy to tragedy – in Goldsmith's terms, from the garden to the grave. Sean Thornton's return to Ireland is not motivated by a touristic impulse but by a therapeutic quest to undo the effects of trauma, brought about by his killing of an opponent in the boxing ring. In Chapter 2,

I argue that such resolution as is achieved at the end of the film is not through 'the talking cure' of conventional therapy, or the narrative coherence of a happy ending. In fact, it is difficult to find any narrative coherence at all in *The Quiet Man*. As Richard Neupert notes, the ostensible narrator of the film, Father Lonergan, seems to think that the resolution of Sean and Mary Kate's disagreement over the dowry, and the prospect of a 'happily ever after' marriage, is sufficient to bring the film to a close, and announces this in his voice-over at the end. However, this formulaic Hollywood ending overlooks the wider problem of communal recognition, and specifically Catholic/Protestant relations, which the film then proceeds to address in what appears to be an afterthought tacked on at the end. As Neupert describes it, the creation of Sean and Mary Kate as a happy couple, and the purging of Sean's tragic past, is not resolved 'until Sean has won the respect of everyone in Innisfree by proving himself rightfully part of the Danaher clan':

> Thus Sean's real victory does not occur until he has defeated Will, 'the best man in Innisfree'. In addition, the fight proves that Sean has overcome his traumatic fear of fighting brought on by killing his last opponent. Thus Sean's return to Ireland has been a *cure* forcing him to recover from having killed a man in the ring as a prizefighter. Sean learns that Ireland expects fights too, but here they are fought for very different reasons and rewards; instead of money, fighting in Ireland earns him a wife, land and community.[24]

It is thus not the talking but the *social* cure – the reclaiming by Sean of his sundered history and community – that lifts the shadow of his American past. But it would be mistaken to see this as simply an uncritical acceptance of tradition, as a reversion to an ethnicity unsullied by change or a critical exchange between cultures. Many commentators have drawn attention to the role of custom in exposing the myth of unfettered individualism which Sean brings with him from America, but more astute critics see in the film a contestation of tradition, especially as it affects the subjugation of women. Irish viewers in particular have expressed their disapproval and unease at the physical abuse of Mary Kate when Sean drags her back through the fields from the station, and more specifically the scene where an older woman hands Sean a stick 'to beat the lovely lady with'.[25] Such responses, however, fail to register the intricate narrative undoing of this 'custom' at the end of the film. It is this reversal which leads Brandon French to conclude that it is not only the 'outsider', Sean, but also the 'insider', Mary Kate, who questions an unthinking conformity to tradition:

> Her break with tradition is epitomized at the end of the film when Mary Kate tosses away the stick which an old woman gave Sean to keep his wife in line. In doing so, Mary Kate rejects the notion of her husband's mastery, to which the older woman has obviously acquiesced.[26]

If there is anything more stereotypical than the characters in *The Quiet Man*, it is the responses of critics who take the film entirely at face value and see in it only the surface simplicity that Sean Thornton himself mistakes for the real Ireland. It may have been with Brandon French's feminist reading in mind that one-time Ford admirer Richard Schickel singles out *The Quiet Man* for scathing criticism in his reappraisal of Ford as a director:

> Buried inside there is, as some critics have noted, a parable about a woman's need to assert her independence that is particularly brave in the film's context – tradition bound Ireland of the 1920s. But that idea is swamped by the movie's shameless Irishry: comic drunkenness, another epic brawl and the brutalization of its heroine, Maureen O'Hara, played for laughs. Indeed, all of Irish life is viewed with a cunning, sentimental twinkle in the eye. Far from being the genial

travelogue Ford thought it was, it is among the most witless and vulgar movies ever made by a supposed major director.[27]

In what follows, I attempt to show that almost every aspect of the film, from Sean's arrival at the station to the final curtain call to the audience, is framed in such a way – whether by the camera, the narrative structure, the *mise-en-scène*, the set design or the script – as to raise questions over what exactly it is we are seeing, and where reality ends and imagination begins. Ford's irony, humour and over-the-top treatment should be sufficient by itself to place much of what we see in *The Quiet Man* between the visual equivalent of inverted commas. The depiction of stereotypes, romantic escapism or nostalgic sentiment is not of itself an endorsement of them, any more than the portrayal of Ethan Edward's (John Wayne) Indian-hating pathology in *The Searchers* an espousal of racism. Notwithstanding the imposing outdoor locations in Ford's westerns or later Irish films, it is often forgotten that Ford is pre-eminently an expressionist

Plate 6.   The 'real' Quiet Man cottage in Maam valley.

director, and that entire sequences in his film are to be understood as tinged with a subjective or a specific cultural colouring. Depictions of Native Americans in key episodes of *The Searchers* – for example, when Ethan discovers the deranged female captives in the Indian reservation – often say more about the hero and his prejudices than about the Comanche themselves. By the same token, as we shall see, much of what passes for Ireland in *The Quiet Man* is filtered through Sean's nostalgic sensibility and the clash of viewpoints on Irish society with which he has to contend. When Michaeleen Oge Flynn points out, in response to Sean's first enchanted view of White O'Morn, 'Ah, that's nothing but a wee humble cottage,' it is not obvious that he has any greater grasp of the truth than Sean. In the end, the achievement of the film may be to bring out precisely this tension between 'the real', in the sense of the actual and the matter of fact, and the 'real', in the very different sense of authenticity and value – with home lying somewhere in the shadows in between.

1

MAURICE WALSH: THE WRITER

One afternoon in the early 1960s, Jack Hemingway, the son of the famous writer, walked into the bar in the Algonquin Hotel in New York, an old haunt of his father's, expecting to meet up with some writers. To his disappointment, he found that the bar was virtually empty except for two men arguing passionately at a table in the corner. At a particularly heated moment, one of the figures – 'a red-faced, white-haired man' – thumped the table declaring: 'The greatest storyteller of them all was Ernest Hemingway.' Taking his cue, the younger Hemingway went over and introduced himself, suggesting that he perhaps was in a position to clear up the argument:

> 'I'm sure you gentlemen will be interested to know that he often talked to me about that very question: Who is the greatest storyteller of them all? He was very certain whom it was. He was a writer you gentlemen may not have heard of! The greatest storyteller of them all, my father used to say, was an Irish writer called Maurice Walsh.'
> 'Oh, my Christ!' said the white-haired man. 'I'm Maurice Walsh.'[28]

Maurice Walsh, the author of the short story on which *The Quiet Man* was based, was born into a comfortable farming background at Lisselton, near Listowel, County Kerry, in 1879, and spent most of his working life as a Customs and Excise officer, first in the Scottish Highlands and subsequently, with the founding of the Irish Free State, in Dublin. In the course of his duties in the Highlands, Walsh became an enthusiast for the outdoor life, and set-pieces drawing on his love of fishing, hunting and horse-riding pervade his fiction. He also acquired a reputation as a connoisseur of whisky, if we are to believe J. Marshall Robb in his *Scotch Whisky: a Survey*:

Plate 7. *Maurice Walsh.*

I knew one small town [in Scotland] with seven distilleries and I knew an expert [i.e. Walsh] who could distinguish the seven by bouquet alone. The seven distilleries were in one mile of highland river; they used the same water, peat and malt, and the methods of brewing and distillation were identical, yet each spirit had its own individual bouquet. One, the best, mellowed perfectly in seven years; another, the least good, not a hundred yards away, was still liquid fire at the end of ten years.[29]

As Steve Matheson writes in his biography of Walsh, something of this ability to discern nuances and shades of difference was carried over into his relationship with nature and the environment, leading to the almost mystical sense of place which he attached to landscape: 'A place acquires an entity of its own, an entity that is the essence of all the life and thoughts and griefs and joys that have gone before.'[30] This deep emotional investment in land, converting property into a territorial archive of the community, pervades his romantic fiction, whether it functions as a national or, as in the case of *The Quiet Man*, a personal or family inheritance.

As his date of birth indicates, Walsh was born into an Irish countryside convulsed by the upheavals of the Land War, and though he liked to describe himself as 'son of John Walsh, farmer and Land Leaguer', his father, in fact, was pro-British in outlook, thus setting him at odds with his son's burgeoning nationalist sentiments. Maurice Walsh's early political sympathies did not prevent him – like many before him – from entering the British Civil Service, notwithstanding his support for the Boers and his detestation of what he described as 'the bloody Empire'. On returning to Dublin in 1922 as part of the new state-building effort, he was posted to the Phoenix Park Distillery at Chapelizod, formerly the workplace of John Stanislaus Joyce, father of James Joyce. It was during this period that Walsh found his vocation as a writer, his first novel, *The Key Above the Door* (1926), set in the

Scottish Highlands, becoming a bestseller. This earned him a highly laudatory encomium from J. M. Barrie which helped to further promote his career, and in 1932 he had a second major popular success with *Blackcock's Feather*, an adventure story set in Elizabethan Ireland. It is not clear when Walsh's prowess as a storyteller came to the attention of Hemingway, but John Ford's acquaintance with the Kerry writer can be dated to the publication of the story 'The Quiet Man' in the popular American magazine, the *Saturday Evening Post*, on 11 February 1933. This proved to be a financial breakthrough for Walsh, earning him $2,000 and introducing his fiction to the lucrative American market. The timing was salutary, for in 1933, due to severe cutbacks in public sector pay introduced by the new de Valera government, Walsh felt compelled to resign from the Civil Service, thus making him more dependent on his earnings as a writer. Following its appearance in the *Saturday Evening Post*, John Ford set about buying the rights to 'The Quiet Man' and in February 1936 entered into an agreement paying initially a mere $10 for the exclusive rights to the story, and a further $2,500 plus half the excess of that figure if the story was sold to a film company. By this time, Walsh had reworked and expanded the story, integrating it into a sequence of five interconnected stories, *Green Rushes* (1935), set during the Black and Tan period of the War of Independence and its aftermath.

'A False Peace'

An hour or two ago we has been strung to kill, and here, now, we were lazying in a valley of peace – though it was a false peace . . . quiet men all, quiet as this valley below the hills.

Maurice Walsh, *Green Rushes*, 1935[31]

Green Rushes belongs to the genre of romantic or adventure fiction associated with Robert Louis Stevenson (with whom Walsh was often compared) or popularized in Walsh's own time by writers such as

John Buchan. The emphasis on plot, action and setting carries the stories along rather than the complexities of character or inner life, and crises are resolved through public showdowns or confrontations, more often than not in fist-fights. Time and again, characters in *Green Rushes* turn out to be prizefighters with a past, or trained boxers, which certainly facilitates the 'fight to the finish' on which the stories end. It is perhaps no coincidence, either, that the narrative formula of westerns often lies in the background of these personal duels, and that the central characters in no less than three of the five stories are visiting or returned Americans from the frontiers of Arizona, New Mexico or Canada: 'Owen Jordan, [medical] doctor to the Flying Column, Irish-American, and son of a Fenian', in Part One, 'Then Came the Captain's Daughter'; Paddy Bawn Enright, in Part Three, 'The Quiet Man' (transformed into Sean Thornton in the film version); and the dubious Art O'Connor, suspected of being a British-Canadian spy, in Part Four, 'The Red Girl'. This undoubtedly helped American readers identify with the stories, not least John Ford, who had already established his reputation as a director of westerns.

The influence of not so much the American as the Irish wilderness is also present in the outdoor locations of the stories, as characters are constantly framed against a landscape evoked by lush descriptions of nature or scenery. This conveys a bucolic atmosphere even in the midst of conflict, with feared leaders of IRA flying columns fraternizing on the most cordial terms with British army officers, sharing the pleasures of fishing and hunting as they patrol the Irish countryside. In this world, terrorism is often indistinguishable from tourism and it is hardly surprising that political antagonisms seemingly fade into the background, eclipsed by personal entanglements or affairs of the heart:

> And here we were now, hoping for a quiet month amongst the hill-farmers: fishing a little, sleeping deeply, gathering a fresh store of munitions, experimenting with land-mines cunningly contrived out of railway buffers, girding ourselves

> for a fresh sally to the endless and careful fighting ...
> (Walsh, p. 19)

The only villains are the Black and Tans and perhaps the double-dealing English spies: in the opening story, 'Then Came the Captain's Daughter', both the IRA and respectable British officers seek to distance themselves from the Black and Tan rabble terrorizing the neighbourhood. The idealized picture of intimate enemies is not entirely implausible, as the narrative is at pains to point out that Hugh Forbes (the Tom Barry-like character who leads the IRA column), Sean Glynn, the IRA intelligence officer, and the Scottish army captain, Archie MacDonald, were friends in the British army during the Great War. In John Ford's '1921', the final instalment of *The Rising of the Moon* (1957), there is a similar distancing of the acceptable face of colonial rule from the Black and Tans, as the RIC (Royal Irish Constabulary) policeman barely conceals his hostility towards their crude methods, and the British major in charge of the execution of the rebels is almost on the side of the nationalists, exclaiming: 'Four years of war and I end up a hangman. How much longer are they going to keep us here?'

In Walsh's story, this camaraderie among equals fails to account, however, for the equally idealized picture of the welcome extended to the British army in the Irish countryside, the impression being given at times that the role of the gentlemanly 'real' army was to protect the locals from the rough justice of the Black and Tans. In one scene set in a bar in the opening story, the hotheaded Black and Tan Garner is manhandling Owen Jordan, the Irish-American narrator of the story who has joined the IRA flying column, when the benign Captain MacDonald walks in:

> 'What's this, Garner?'
> 'Shinners – IRA killers, Captain.'
> 'You know?'
> 'Whispering, heads together – in there –'

'That all?'

'Molouney is under suspicion – and this fellow –'

The officer was close to him now. 'You're drunk, man. You can't treat men this way.'

'The –'

'Not while I command.'

His voice was still quiet, but I still could sense the hot Scots devil behind it.

'I will deal with this, Garner.'

'They'll plug you in the back.'

'They've had many opportunities. Go back to barracks! Do you hear? I'm in command here. Go!' (Walsh, p. 24)

This compliment is, as it were, returned later when the men of Hugh Forbes' flying column wait in ambush for an approaching Black and Tan patrol and call off their attack when Captain MacDonald and his red-haired sister, Margaid, are spotted in the leading car. This leads to their falling into the hands of the rebels – amongst whom are their erstwhile friends, Hugh Forbes and Sean Glynn – and the rest of the story revolves around their rather amiable experiences as hostages in the picturesque surroundings of north Kerry, culminating in a romance between Owen Jordan and the attractive Margaid – 'a small and lonely bit of a girl set here amongst us in a tortured land, fishing carefree in a false peace' (Walsh, p. 35).[32]

For all the pastoral fantasy in *Green Rushes*, it is this theme of a 'false peace' which introduces a sinister note into the surface pleasantry of the stories and gives the lie to the comforting illusions of the rural idyll. Venting his unease at Captain MacDonald's rash decision to bring his sister out into the war-torn countryside, Owen Jordan muses:

Her brother was a dashed fool ever to bring her here. His was a peaceful area [i.e. the district under the Captain's control], indeed, thanks mostly to his own understanding of

> the breed, but that understanding should have told him that
> the peace was a false one and might shatter at any hour – as
> it was shattered now, though this girl did not know it yet.
> (Walsh, p. 35)

Though the well-disposed Captain understands 'the breed', he misses a crucial aspect of the apparent composure of the countryside that is not lost on his more abrasive Black and Tan counterpart, Garner. It is, in fact, the deceptiveness of the surface consensus of the countryside, the pretence of acquiescence to British rule that was really only a matter of waiting for the right opportunity to strike, that brings the highly-strung Garner to the verge of breakdown, as indicated by his suspicion of even people whispering in a pub described above:

> That man, set to subdue a people not easily subduable, had
> been subject to months of constant strain . . . It was a people
> quietly inimical, wearing submissiveness as a mask, bearing
> abuse calmly, biding its own time . . . The strain of waiting,
> the strain of watching, the deadly explosiveness below the
> deadly calm, had brought this man to the breaking-point.
> (Walsh, p. 23)

As it turns out, there is indeed a deadly, almost Gothic, incident at the heart of *Green Rushes* which frames the entire five stories even though it barely surfaces in the action. The book opens with a prologue which relates how the seductively beautiful Nuala O'Carroll from Tipperary – her love of Ireland matched only by her love of horses – meets a fellow patriot Martin Kierley, who has a taste for the finer life and an endless capacity to spend money. They marry, fall on hard times, but then during the Troubles the money starts to flow again and comes to the attention of her cousin (and secret admirer) Sean Glynn, head of IRA intelligence in the area. At the same time, the IRA begin to suspect the existence of an informer in their ranks and ask Glynn to persuade Nuala Kierley to use her beguiling looks to seduce a British spy and find out the source of the leak. This she does, only to discover that the traitor is her husband. He pleads that it was for her and their lifestyle he took the money, but she disowns him – 'she cared for him too. But there and then she spurned him, would have nothing to do with him, would not let him touch her, would never forgive a traitor. In the end he saw that' (Walsh, p. 10). He is taken prisoner by the IRA but escapes from custody in an old haunted ruin on the very night the Treaty was signed, 'and, next morning, was found drowned in *Poul Cailin Rua* – the Red Girl's Pool – which is the pool of traitors . . . And then Nuala Kierley disappeared and no friend set eyes on her for seven years' (Walsh, p. 10).

The suggestion in the story is that Nuala has fallen into a life of ill-repute and it is subsequently revealed that her seductive beauty ensnared not only her ill-fated husband but also Sean Glynn, the IRA intelligence officer, who fell for her charms and thus strayed from the attentions of his intended, Joan Hyland. The second story of *Green Rushes*, 'Over the Border', is set years after the War of Independence and deals with the return of Major (as he is now) MacDonald to the district to meet up with his old friend, Sean Glynn, who has fallen prey to alcoholism following his affair with Nuala Kierley and his break-up with Joan. Through the Major's good efforts – and with a little bit of help from his friend Paddy Bawn Enright – Sean and Joan are reconciled, but not before the shadow of betrayal and death in the form of Nuala Kierley again hangs over the story. Paddy Bawn puts his arm on the shoulder of the Major (the narrator of the story) and announces his intention to retire to a life of peace:

> 'Everything will be all right now – and my own little place waiting for me up on Knockanure Hill.'
> But [the Major muses] a strange thought still obsessed me.
> Suddenly I felt extraordinarily bitter.

'They are all right in there,' I said, 'and you are all right too, Paddy Bawn, but what about Nuala Kierley? The broken one! Who thinks of her?'

'You do,' said Paddy Bawn.

'Because I am sorry for her.'

'God help her – and you too!' (Walsh, p. 114)

'The Quiet Man'

It is at this point that Part Three of *Green Rushes*, 'The Quiet Man', picks up the thread of the narrative, elaborating on the shorter version published in the *Saturday Evening Post* which had first attracted Ford's interest.[33] Shawn Kelvin in the original story becomes Paddy Bawn Enright in *Green Rushes*, who in turn is transformed into Sean Thornton in Ford's film. Many aspects of Paddy Bawn are carried over into the characterization of Sean Thornton in the film, the most prominent being:

(i)   he is a returned emigrant who has worked in the steel furnaces of Pittsburgh, and who settles in a 'four-roomed, lime-white, thatched cottage' (Walsh, p. 117);

(ii) he has a past in professional boxing;

(iii) he has a love of horses, both for hunting and jumping;

(iv) his antagonist in the local community is the brutish Red Will O'Danaher (simply 'Danaher' in the film), land-grabber and 'rancher';

(v)   Paddy Bawn's troublesome marriage to Red Will's sister, the red-haired Ellen Roe ('Mary Kate' in the film), is permitted because Red Will believes getting her out of the house is necessary for his own marriage prospects with the Widow Carey ('Widow Tillane' in the film);

(vi) Paddy Bawn's visitations to the church provide him with a pretext to admire Ellen Roe;

(vii) the frustration of Red Will's designs on the widow and the unresolved question of Ellen Roe's dowry become the points of conflict around which the action revolves; and

(viii) the resolution of the conflict takes the form of a fist-fight on Red Will's farm in front of the local community, and a threshing machine into whose fire-box Paddy Bawn throws the contested dowry.

In the published story, however, the Enright family farm has been taken over during Paddy Bawn's stay in the United States by O'Danaher and, we are told, 'no one, in living memory, remembered an Irishman who had taken the loss of his land quietly – not since the Fenian times at any rate' (Walsh, p. 115). Paddy Bawn's initial reluctance to challenge Red Will is attributed by his gossipy neighbours to the fact that, unlike Sean Thornton, he is a smallish man (a welterweight boxer 'below medium height', but described as a 'little Yankee runt' by Red Will) and thus is at a physical disadvantage. This brings the prospect of additional shame and communal opprobrium on the returned emigrant, providing an important incentive for regaining his pride in the showdown with Red Will that is missing in the film. Added to this is the fact that Ellen Roe is pregnant with their first child, which she discloses at a propitious moment when Paddy Bawn backs down from what he considers an ignominious pursuit of her dowry:

'Woman, woman!' he said in his deep voice. 'Why would you and I shame ourselves like this?'

'Shame!' she cried. 'Will you let him shame you now?'

'But your own brother, Ellen – before them all –?'

'And he cheating you –'

'God's glory, woman!' His voice was distressed and angry too. 'What is his dirty money to me? Are you a Danaher after all?'

That stung her, and she stung him back with one final hurting effort. She placed a hand below her breast, and looked close into his face. Her voice was low and bitter.

'I am a Danaher. It is a great pity that the father of this, my son, is an Enright coward.' (Walsh, p. 129)[34]

The motivation for the escalating conflict between Paddy Bawn and Red Will is thus more varied and intrinsic to the community than in Ford's film. The reason for this is clear in that, unlike Sean Thornton, Paddy Bawn is depicted as having returned from the United States some years before, and is successfully integrated into the social life of the locality. His dream of retirement from prizefighting to a quiet rural life is shattered, however, in a way that perhaps marks the most profound difference between the story and the film:

> The truth was that he had had enough of fighting. All he wanted now was peace – 'a quiet small little place on a hillside' . . . And yet, for the best part of five years Paddy Bawn Enright did not enjoy one quiet day in that quiet place. The horror and the dool [i.e. 'dhoul' – darkness] of the Black and Tan war settled down on Ireland, and Paddy Bawn, driven by an ideal bred closer in the bone of an Irishman than all desire, went out to fight against the terrible thing that England stood for in Ireland – the subjugation of the soul. He joined an IRA fighting column, a column great amongst all the flying columns of the south, commanded by Hugh Forbes, with Mickeen Oge Flynn second in command; and with that column he fought and marched until the truce came. (Walsh, p. 116)

It may not be too difficult to imagine John Wayne, in the role of Sean Thornton, fighting for Irish freedom, for Wayne had built his reputation as a star on such action roles, whether in westerns or in classic war movies such as *Back to Bataan* (dir. Edward Dmytryk, 1945). But to imagine Barry Fitzgerald – Michaeleen Oge Flynn in the film – as the second-in-command of the flying column calls for an exercise in imagination of a different order.[35] The incongruity is even greater when we learn from one of the characters in *Green Rushes* that Mickeen Oge is a great reader and scholar: 'I have been through your library you know – travel, literature, sport, chemistry, and a great ugly pile of dry theology.' 'I am known as a spoilt priest,' comes the reply (Walsh, p. 160) – one aspect of Mickeen Oge's character that is not, perhaps, inconsistent with his black-frocked impish persona in the film.

In the fourth story of *Green Rushes*, 'The Red Girl', Mickeen Oge Flynn picks up a visiting American stranger, Art O'Connor, having missed him at the railway station, and takes him on a jaunt through the countryside in a scene reminiscent of the opening episode of *The Quiet Man*:

> As they rattled along the uphill road winding below the curving brow breasts of the hills, this American, Art O'Connor, was thinking to himself. So this serious-faced man in rough tweeds was the Mickeen Oge Flynn that his partner, Owen Jordan, talked so much about. Great guerrilla fighter, hunger striker, incorruptible republican – and now driving a flivver for an angler's hotel. Some comedown in the world. Perhaps only a blind! (Walsh, p. 146)[36]

The implication running throughout the later stories of *Green Rushes* is that, even though the hostilities of the War of Independence and the Civil War have ceased and a tranquillity of sorts has fallen over the countryside, the struggle is far from over and Mickeen Oge, for one, has not given up the fight. The story 'The Red Girl' turns on the suspicion that Art O'Connor – from Canada, not the United States – is a British spy intent on uncovering caches of republican arms, and the red girl in the title of the story alludes to the ancient legend of a red-haired woman who haunts a pool near the ruins of Castle Aonach where the arms are hidden. When his uncle reveals that O'Connor is from Montreal, Mickeen Oge replies:

> 'Montreal! That's Canada – that's the British Empire. We'll keep an eye on him.'
> 'Have sense, man! What the hell has the British Empire to do with us now?'
> 'As long as Ireland is not free – aye! and when it is – the British secret service will occasionally run its hand over us. A great empire, uncle, and its agents never sleep.' He moved across to the door. 'Leave the back door on the latch – I may be late.'
> 'Be careful now, Mickeen Oge!' warned his uncle seriously. (Walsh, p. 151)

Unlike the film, Paddy Bawn's first view of Red Will's sister is in church, but the apparition of the mysterious Red Girl to Art O'Connor in the succeeding story has more in common with the famous scene in the film when Sean Thornton's eyes first alight on Mary Kate Danaher, walking through the fields:

> I turned around then and looked up – up there. And there, leaning on the wall, was the woman – no ghost woman; flesh and blood, or I have no eyes to see – the sun shining on her red hair, and her scarf green as grass on her shoulders. She was not looking at me. She was looking over my head at the far side of the pool . . . I only saw her over my shoulder but she was fit to sit with the Mona Lisa amongst the rocks – more beautiful by far and no less wicked. A woman I never saw before, yet a woman strangely familiar – like a face out of a secret dream, perhaps the dream of the race, God save us! (Walsh, p. 164)

This apparition evokes not just the Mona Lisa but, in an Irish context, 'the dream of the race', the visionary figure of the *speirbhean* ('sky-woman') in eighteenth-century *aisling* ('dream') poetry, a fairy woman who appears in woods or natural surroundings to an unsuspecting male, promising deliverance from political oppression and a return of the Jacobite or Stuart monarchy. Echoes of the vanished Stuart dynasty – the archetypal vision of an idealized, Gaelic Ireland before 'the Fall' brought about by the Williamite conquest – recur throughout *Green Rushes*, and in the opening story the legend of the mysterious Red Girl who is 'fatal to all renegades' (Walsh, p. 43) is related to the 'strange sadness' of the tune the *Lon Dubh* ('The Blackbird') – 'a dance tune, one of the hard long dances, and besides, it is the only Irish lament for the Stuart kings' (Walsh, p. 48). In the fourth story, described above, the apparition is, in fact, a hoax and is staged, using a red wig and green scarf, to keep the spying Art O'Connor from probing too close to Mickeen Oge's arms cache in Castle Aonach.

Many of the different strands in the earlier stories, including the dark mystery of 'the Red Girl's pool', are brought together in the final story, 'Bad Town Dublin', set in the city rather than the countryside. It transpires that the traitor Martin Kierley, whose tale of woe was recounted in the prologue, was mysteriously drowned in the Red Girl's Pool, and in the final episode of the book his enigmatic wife Nuala, who had brought him to his doom, reappears as a shadowy actress in Dublin, the living incarnation of a woman 'fatal to all renegades'. Though he caught a glimpse of this femme fatale when he was held as a hostage by Sean Glynn and his IRA column, Major MacDonald does not realize her identity on meeting her again in Dublin until he attends a play in the Gaiety Theatre with his former captor (and Nuala's erstwhile lover), Sean Glynn. When Sean admits that 'the thought of her nearly drove me mad once, as you know,' the Major replies:

[That was] because we dramatized her – from the very beginning. That was why I did not recognize her at once this afternoon. She was the wandering woman, Erin – wandering, forlorn, defeated, but never lost. And she is only a minor actress in a second-rate English play. (Walsh, p. 195)

Nuala, then, like the visionary Red Girl, is the mythic archetype of Mother Ireland or, perhaps, her more sexually alluring daughters, 'Dark Rosaleen' or 'Cathleen ni Houlihan'. In her 'fallen' condition, however, Nuala is on the verge of marrying the former English spy and boxer, Sir Henry Hanley, who was the paymaster of her informer husband. In what might be seen as an Irish version of a 'captivity narrative', she is rescued and is shepherded off to the Irish countryside to live under the protection of Paddy Bawn Enright, but, on returning to Dublin to take part in the Horse Show, has to be rescued once more from Hanley's clutches when Paddy Bawn's superior boxing skills win out in the final showdown.

Terror Recollected in Tranquillity

Though *Green Rushes* is haunted by an almost primordial act of violence committed during the War of Independence, this is, for the most part, suppressed and removed to the margins of the interwoven stories in the book, along with other, more sordid aspects of the conflict. When Paddy Bawn settles down with Ellen Roe in 'The Quiet Man', he begins to share with her his memories of the ironworks in Pittsburgh – 'he made her see the glare of molten metal lambent yet searing, made her feel the sucking heat, made her feel the clang' (Walsh, p. 124) – and also revisits his days in the ring as a prizefighter – 'she could picture the roped square under the dazzle of the hooded arcs, with the updrifting smoke layer above. . . she came to understand the explosive restraint of the game' (Walsh, p. 124). But while these relatively discomfiting episodes of the past can be recollected in tranquillity, the same does not apply to the traumatic legacies of the war: 'But they did not speak at all of the Black and Tan war. That was too near them. That made men frown and women shiver' (Walsh, p. 124). The silence that lies at the heart of 'The Quiet Man', then, is essentially political in nature – the human equivalent of the 'false peace' which lulls the countryside into a deceptive sense of security. When the suggestion is made in the following story, 'The Red Girl', that it was most likely Mickeen Oge and his comrades, rather than the 'unquiet spirit' of the phantom Red Girl, who was responsible for the drowning of the traitor Martin Kierley in *Poul Cailín Rua* (The Red Girl's Pool), one of the characters, the young Englishwoman Betty Caverley, protests that Mickeen Oge would never carry out such a dishonourable deed, but she later reflects on his silent ways:

> He was not old . . . But of course he had suffered . . . She knew of his fight in the Black and Tan and the civil war, of his internment, his terrible hunger strike, his escape, his campaign in the hills . . . But she could never get him to talk of those experiences . . . A strange, calm, gentle man . . . in a strange land – and the strangest thing of all was that a man might be working humbly, and yet be one of his land's chosen men . . . And he could be so deeply silent. (Walsh, p. 158)

The impression given throughout *Green Rushes* is that surface calm belies the turbulence and violence underneath, as if the whole semblance of pastoral was designed to efface – or displace – the terror secreted in the landscape. 'You know,' says the former IRA intelligence officer Sean Glynn, when he hears about the re-appearance of his ex-lover Nuala Kierley in Dublin, 'a thing once done will never let you go. Nuala and I once did a thing together, and it holds us still – here tonight its claws are in us' (Walsh, p. 196).

While there are many points of detail, as we have seen, on which the film adaptation departs from the original story, the central continuity between Maurice Walsh's book and Ford's *The Quiet Man* relates to an attempt by the central character to throw off the shadow of a traumatic event in the past. As such, the film draws not just on the specific story of 'The Quiet Man' but on the overall Gothic theme of a dark secret that has been consigned to silence, but not to oblivion. In the film, however, the further reduction of the political content of the story – where it is all but reduced to a series of asides

– presented Ford's scriptwriter, Frank Nugent, with a problem in accounting for the hero's taciturn silence over his past and his need to regain his pride through his ritualistic combat with Red Will. Nugent's solution was to transfer the original traumatic violent event from a *political* to a *personal* past – from the buried communal memory of north Kerry during the Troubles to Sean Thornton's deep-seated guilt over having killed an opponent in the ring in America. This pivotal shift in the substance of the story seems to have been lost on the copywriter for the dust-jacket of the Irish paperback edition of *Green Rushes* (retitled *The Quiet Man* to capitalize on the success of the film). Here we are informed in relation to central protagonist Paddy Bawn Enright:

> He was called the Quiet Man, and he was that, although he had played a man's part in the Black and Tan War. His ideal was to settle down on the side of Knockanore Hill and watch life go by; and he did that and then the past came back. In his time he had been one of the most terrible two-fisted fighters in the American ring. One man had never recovered from the punishment dealt out in one furious round. That day he threw his gloves away and resolved, under no circumstances, to fight again. Under no compulsion would he fight any man – but the compulsion was there bearing down on his whole life, on his love . . .

In fact, it is not just the title but also the story of the film that has been borrowed for the back cover of the paperback edition. There is no mention in the original story of killing an opponent in the ring, or of hanging up the gloves afterwards in remorse – this is introduced into the screenplay precisely to compensate for the absence of the politically inspired tragedy haunts the original book.

Though it is displaced, the political dimension, as we shall see in the next chapter, is not entirely absent from Ford's film. Such is the power of the gruesome flashback to Sean's violent past in the ring, for instance, that it seems to be charged with the Gothic horror of the original Irish setting. Though the other stories in *Green Rushes* do not figure directly in Nugent's screenplay, residues and traces from them are discernible throughout the film. One of the most notable borrowings is the cryptic gesture at the end of the film where Mary Kate whispers coyly into Sean's Thornton's ear; this recalls an incident in the opening story of *Green Rushes* in which Margaid MacDonald turns to her admirer, Owen Jordan, as she is about to leave Castletown:

> The [pony] trap is down,' she said calmly, 'and you and I are inside. I am not going.'
> 'No?'
> 'No. Listen, you poor stubborn simpleton.' She laid her two fine hands on my shoulder and drew my head closer. 'Let me whisper in your ear.'
> That whisper is a secret of my own. (Walsh, p. 69)

The story of John Ford's film also turns on a secret: a hidden truth brought out into the open and worked through in public – while still remaining concealed from the community – which enables Sean Thornton, 'The Quiet Man', to lift the shadow from his past.

2

NOSTALGIA AND NATIONAL ROMANCE

....

A bucolic comedy, The Quiet Man *seemed destined to break the spell of combat. . . but it is no less haunted by violence and social disruption than the films which preceded it.*
Joseph McBride and Michael Wilmington, *John Ford,* 1974[37]

Among the stranger credits for *The Quiet Man* – including 'Censorship: Steve Goodman', 'Technical Adviser (Religion): Father Stack SJ' and 'Weather Information: US Weather Bureau' (for a film shot in Ireland) – is 'IRA Consultant: Ernie O'Malley'. Had the film sought to incorporate Ernie O'Malley's exploits as an IRA leader during the War of Independence, or the narrative and stylistic verve he displayed in his remarkable memoirs of the period, *On Another Man's Wound* (1936),[38] then the combination of Ford and O'Malley would have made for a landmark film of a different kind. O'Malley, born in County Mayo where *The Quiet Man* was shot, was a key military strategist in the IRA and became assistant Chief of Staff of the Irregular (anti-Treaty) forces during the Civil War. Disillusioned with the new Free State, he emigrated to the United States in 1926 and subsequently moved back and forth between Ireland and the European mainland, striking up friendships with writers such as Hart Crane, Robinson Jeffers and Samuel Beckett, and the photographers Edward Weston and Paul Strand, as well as amassing a considerable private collection of modern art. O'Malley did show up on the set every day during the shooting of *The Quiet Man*, but his role as adviser had more to do with getting the details right about locations and local customs than with political or military matters. According to Maureen O'Hara, John Ford 'had a great deal of respect for Ernie

. . . They would natter away like old buddies . . . They liked each other. They were friends.'[39] As a man of action, O'Malley led the kind of life that Ford would have liked to live himself and was keen to identify with in his own personal accounts of 'the Troubles' in Ireland. During the filming of *The Quiet Man*, Ford arranged for the cast to take part in a fund-raising concert at the Seapoint Ballroom in Salthill, Galway, for the 'County Galway Volunteer Memorial Fund' and, explaining this political turn on the set, related how thirty years earlier he had, quite literally, a walk-on part in the dramatic events that led to the founding of the state.[40]

On Friday morning, 2 December 1921, Arthur Griffith travelled to Dublin with the contentious 'Proposed Articles of Agreement' for the Treaty. Michael Collins stayed behind for two further meetings on financial matters at the Treasury and, with Erskine Childers and George Gavan Duffy, caught the mail train at Euston that evening at 8.45, to sail to Ireland on the mailboat from Holyhead. Collins's aim was to be in Dublin early next morning to allow him time to consult with senior IRB members before attending the crucial cabinet meeting with de Valera at 11.00 a.m. Collins and his party boarded the *Cambria* on schedule, but shortly after midnight the mailboat was in a fatal collision with a fishing schooner sailing from Liverpool, the *James Tyrell*. Three men from the fishing vessel lost their lives, but the mailboat was able to save four more, having circled around for some time. As marine historians Jim Rees and Liam Charlton recount, two well-dressed strangers visited the survivors during the night, the tallest of the strangers lighting a cigarette for the schooner's eighteen-year-old engineer. It was only when the stranger had departed, leaving the rest of the packet of cigarettes behind him, that the young engineer was informed he had been visited by Michael Collins.[41]

John Ford sailed from New York to Liverpool in late November 1921 and boarded the *Cambria* at Holyhead on the same night. In a letter written to his wife Mary in December 1921, he gives a graphic account of the disastrous night's crossing:

As soon as I landed in Liverpool I left for Ireland. The boat I travelled in across the Irish Sea carried Michael Collins and Arthur Griffith [*sic*], the returning Sinn Féin delegates with Lloyd George's proposals to Dáil Éireann. We were only twenty minutes from Holyhead when we cut a fishing schooner in two and sank her. Three of the crew were drowned and although we cruised around for an hour we found no bodies. The shock of the impact was terrible. When we struck, the boat shivered and rocked for quite a while before she straightened out . . .[42]

It was not only the boat that shuddered, for Collins's own nerves must have been jangled when the *Cambria* docked in Dun Laoghaire at 10.15 a.m., leaving him less than an hour to get to what Tim Pat Coogan has described as 'one of the most important cabinet discussions ever conducted by any Irish Political party'.[43] But Ford's troubles were not over either. Arriving in Dublin, he headed west in time-honoured fashion but found that the War of Independence had taken a heavy toll on his family relatives:

At Galway I got a jaunting car and rode to Spiddal and had a deuce of a time finding Dad's folks. There are so many Feeneys out there that to find our part of the family was a problem. At last I found them . . . Spiddal is all shot to pieces. Most of the houses have been burned down by the Black and Tans and all the young men had been hiding in the hills. As it was during the truce that I was there I was unmolested BUT Cousin Martin Feeney (Dad's nephew) had been hiding in the Connemara Mountains with the Thornton boys. I naturally was followed about and watched by the B[lack] and T[an] fraternity. Tell Dad that the Thornton house is entirely burned down and old Mrs Thornton was living with Uncle Ned's widow while his sons were away . . .[44]

This letter is an uncanny anticipation of the opening scenes in *The Quiet Man* in which a returned emigrant, Sean Thornton, casts a melancholy eye on the ruins of the old Thornton cottage, while the words of 'old Mrs Thornton' echo in his memory. Ford is alluding in his letter to the destruction wreaked on Spiddal and its environs in May, 1921, as a reprisal for an IRA attack on the police barracks in the village, the fury of the Black and Tans being particularly directed at the Costello, Thornton and Feeney households, which were burned to the ground.[45] As a contemporary newspaper report described it (Plate 8):

Mr Thornton's house was built only a few years ago, and was unoccupied. About midnight, a bomb was thrown into it, and petrol was sprinkled all about the place. His two sons –

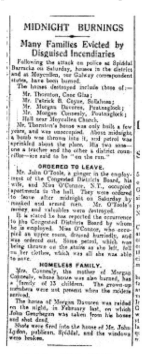

Plate 8. Freeman's Journal, *May 17th, 1921.*

one a teacher, and the other a district councillor – are said to be 'on the run'.[46]

The Feeneys were Ford's immediate family, and the Thorntons were cousins. Martin Thornton, a member of another branch of the Thornton family, was a professional boxer like his fictional counterpart in *The Quiet Man*, his prowess in the ring earning him the name of 'the Connemara Crusher'. In the extended Donnybrook sequence at the end of *The Quiet Man*, Martin Thornton acted as Victor McLaglen's stand-in as he engages in a fight to the finish with John Wayne, thus giving an uncanny real-life provenance to the underlying story of a Thornton fighting with his dark, violent shadow.[47]

Ford did not attempt to bring Ernie O'Malley's exploits to the screen, but, in the immediate aftermath of *The Quiet Man*, he opened up correspondence with another legendary IRA leader Dan Breen with a view to making a docudrama on the life of Kevin Barry:

> All of the characters now living would participate. This would be a grand historical document . . . I have in mind the story of Kevin Barry. This is a patriotic and anti-British theme, but as a showman for many years it has been my belief that the British seem to welcome that sort of thing, viz. 'The Informer', etc. I've talked to Maureen [O'Hara] about it and. . . I think she would throw herself heart and soul behind any project that is as nationalist as this.[48]

This mentality helps to explain, perhaps, the tenor of Ford's draft notes for *The Quiet Man*, which suggest that he intended to integrate a much darker and more explicit sub-plot about the IRA, setting the story not after the Treaty but during the Black and Tan war: 'A blacksmith taking off his apron, putting out the fire in his furnace, puts on his cap, and hastily ties up a bundle, in which we can see three rifles, and departs. . .' This is followed by suggestions that both the curate and the parish priest are involved in the struggle, a subplot which was also deleted but not before leaving cryptic traces in the existing film. Again, following the spirit of the original – and demonstrating Ford's familiarity with recent Irish politics – Michaeleen Oge is described in Ford's draft notes as a survivor of the ill-fated Connacht Rangers mutiny in India in 1920 – the only regiment 'in British history that was neither royal nor loyal'. But in what was perhaps the closest adherence to the depiction of Paddy Bawn in the original story, Ford envisaged Sean Thornton being drawn into the IRA after his wedding, thus forsaking his bride for violence in the manner of *High Noon* (one of the films, as we have seen, with which *The Quiet Man* competed for Best Feature Film at the Oscars in 1952). In Richard Llewellyn's expanded novella, which Ford commissioned as the basis of the screenplay, Sean Burke/Thornton 'dressed with cap and trench coat' emerges from his cottage for a night raid with the flying column:

'I am ready,' says Sean quickly closing the door.

It quickly dissolves into daylight, and the roar of the Crossley lorries, and the coming of the 'Terror' . . .

They raid and search town street.

The men lined up, sixty or seventy.

Their hands and caps in the air.

Short close-ups of this action – women's faces at windows – the masked informer in nondescript mack, and the accusing finger (woman informer).

But no shooting . . .

Perhaps pipe music played in dirge.

This would be effective, and so on to our story of Breede Ruad [i.e. Mary Kate].

She is ploughing alone in the fields, her eyes on the far-off hills.[49]

As Des MacHale suggests, Ford's change of heart and his subsequent playing down of the Troubles may have been due to the sensitivities of the Irish government on the issue, and this may explain the inclusion of 'Censorship' in the credits. Among the notes accompanying the script are the following:

1. 'Following our lengthy discussion with Sean Nunan of External Affairs we thought it would be better to show our phase of the Anglo-Irish War of Liberation (the so-called Troubles) in as brief and as novel a form as possible.'

2. 'The 'Terror' is used briefly for dramatic purpose. The coming of the Armistice. We should again try to get a gay mood into the picture . . . Activity in the fields. Characters that we have seen in the ambush are now making hay . . . The blacksmith puts his rifle away and takes down his fishing rod.'[50]

It may be, however, that Ford himself was somewhat war-weary by the time he came to shoot *The Quiet Man*. Having been injured in World War II, Ford had just returned from production work in Korea for his documentary on the war, *This Is Korea*, when he flew to Ireland in 1951. Tag Gallagher notes of Sean Thornton that he, 'like so many Ford characters (and particularly after World War II), has learned to forget the horrid, violent past, and to return home',[51] but this comment could also apply to Ford himself. Frank Nugent's character sketch of Sean Thornton in his screenplay bears out Gallagher's observation but also suggests that the creation of a violent past in the boxing ring was conceived as a narrative compensation – or substitution – for battle fatigue:

> [He was the] killer of a man in the prize-ring. A different killing this than in the war in which Sean had served. So 'Trooper Thorn' hung up his gloves, counted his ring earnings and bethought himself wistfully of his mother's somewhat idealized recollections of their native Innisfree. Now to Ireland he is returning, a Quiet Man seeking forgetfulness of all the wars of the human spirit.[52]

It is not clear precisely what 'war' Sean has fought in but, as the early drafts show, it was probably the Black and Tan war of which Ford himself, as we have seen, had had first-hand experience.

There are a number of 'wars of the human spirit', then, weighing heavily on *The Quiet Man*, which partly accounts for the sheer force of the violent flashback to Sean's past when it irrupts into the narrative. Nor is it any wonder that Sean also 'should again try to get a gay mood into the picture', and suffuse his vision of Ireland with a nostalgic haze bequeathed by his mother. What we now understand by nostalgia owes its origins precisely to the need for a therapeutic model of the past to alleviate the memory of suffering or oppression. Nostalgia, in this sense, was a product of the rise of Romanticism at the end of the eighteenth century, a set of consoling fictions in which, as Nicholas Dames argues, 'a specific form of traumatic memory is erased in favour of a curative memory'.[53] For all its levity and paddywhackery, *The Quiet Man* bears out the Celtic stereotype that, in Ireland, 'the tear and smile seem twin-born', and comedy is shadowed by tragedy much as the rapid transitions in Ford's editing propel us from light to dark, sunshine to thunderstorms, and from tranquillity to terror.

The Politics of Nostalgia

To reclaim nostalgia *as not only a mode of memory but also a mode of history would mean considering it as a strategy – as a response to social conditions and, in fact, as a form of therapy.*

Nicholas Dames, 'Austen's Nostalgics', 2001[54]

In the late eighteenth and early nineteenth century, a major shift in sensibility took place which transformed nostalgia from a form of (over-)attachment to the past, an almost pathological yearning for home, to a means of letting go, a mode of remembrance which allowed one to escape from the past and its discontents. Nostalgia originally was not simply an evocation of an idealized past, but a very distinctive expression of longing – *nostos*, to return home, *algos*, a painful condition – the desire to restore the sense of belonging that is associated with home, and its psychological moorings in childhood and the maternal. As originally diagnosed in the late eighteenth century, nostalgia was placed alongside conditions such as melancholia, hypochondria and bulimia, and first came to prominence in the 1790s when acute experiences of dislocation and homesickness were identified as causes of desertion in the highly mobile French armies in the aftermath of the Revolution. As described by the physician William Falconer, in 1788:

> This disorder is said to begin with melancholy, sadness, love of solitude, silences, loss of appetite for both solid and liquid food, prostration of strength . . . when the disorder is violent, nothing avails but returning to their own country, which is so powerful an agent in the cure, that the very preparations for the return prove more effectual than anything else.[55]

It is often 'followed by fever and hallucinatory visions of home' and if so, then Sean Thornton can indeed be said to be suffering from acute nostalgia at the beginning of *The Quiet Man*. It is no coincidence that intense attachments to home and place came to be defined as personality disorders at a period when the massive dislocations brought about by empire, revolution and capitalism were making their presence felt in even the most remote regions of the world economy. Mobility, migration and an ability to assimilate into strange (mainly urban) surroundings were essential ingredients of this new social order, which accordingly sought to pathologize forms of belonging that resisted this process. As another expert on insanity, Thomas Arnold, wrote at the end of the eighteenth century:

> The unreasonable fondness for the place of our birth, and for whatever is connected to our native soil, is the offspring

of an unpolished state of society, and not uncommonly the inhabitant of dreary and inhospitable climates, where the chief and almost only blessings, are ignorance and liberty.[56]

Nostalgia thus came to be associated with dreary climates, primitive societies and with the lower orders, all of which were considered to be on abundant display in the Ireland of the colonial imagination.

In the early nineteenth century, nostalgia underwent a fundamental change and passed from being a disorder to being the cure itself. Instead of constituting a set of painful remembrances of uprooting and exile, nostalgia came to be seen as a *remedy* for the experience of dislocation that was becoming endemic to modernity. The only cure for nostalgia in its earlier homesick variant was, in fact, to return home, and physicians expressed satisfaction – and wonder – that even the prospect of return restored the patient to health: 'It is an axiom of eighteenth-century nostalgia that one *can* go home again, and in fact *must* go home.'[57] But with the gradual shift in sensibility that attended the major upheavals at the end of the eighteenth century – the industrial revolution, the revolutionary wars, the expansion of empire – a new form of nostalgia sought to anaesthetize the pain of loss and uprooting by severing the connection with the past as it was actually experienced. Distance, it was found, lent enchantment to the view and, through the healing powers of imagination and hindsight, the past was idealized to the extent that it receded from the present. Memory, then, became a way of disconnecting from, rather than connecting to, the past: 'an evident switch has taken place from memory as productive of trauma or sickness to memory as a source of *pleasure*, as a poignant but harmless dip into reminiscence.'[58] Crucially, there is an experience of trauma in both cases except that, the second time round, dimmed by romantic nostalgia, the past is recreated in the image of a dream-world and wrapped in a golden haze which all but removes the source of pain at the outset. This could, of course, be seen as disavowal and denial, though from another point of view it assumes the guise of progress as if, like a modern-day Orpheus, the backward look towards a scene of distress can only bring grief in its wake.

The most striking – and anomalous – aspect of *The Quiet Man* in the light of the development of modern nostalgia is that it seems to exemplify both modes of memory, notwithstanding the tensions between them:

(i)   on the one hand, there is the earlier form of *pathological* nostalgia with its insistence on actual return, the belief that you can go home again; and

(ii) on the other hand, there is *romantic* or elegiac nostalgia, which tends to imbue the maternal home with the aura that comes from loss and detachment but which is based, as we have seen, on the impossibility of return.

It may be, however, that the contradiction is not so great as it appears, for, while Sean Thornton does romanticize the *Irish* past, there is no attempt to draw a veil over the scene of trauma in America, and it is exposed in all its horror in a flashback at one of the key moments in the film. As we shall see, the cinematic device of flashback, at its most intense, works decidedly against romantic nostalgia in that it prevents any detachment from the past – the scene depicted is all too present, albeit in an unwelcome form. This corresponds to point (i) above, the actual immediacy of return as if America corresponds formally to Ireland in Sean's imagination, though at a darker, more destructive level. By contrast, Ireland is subject precisely to the celebratory glow and wistful longing that is used to cover up a scene of trauma in romantic nostalgia, except there is no overt depiction of such a scene where Ireland is concerned. This suggests once more a formal equivalence between Ireland and America in Sean's imagination, as if the 'Hell' of his American past – for all its vivid and overpowering impact – is a *displacement* of the violence and disruption simmering beneath the surface tranquillity of the Irish landscape. The point here is not that Sean Thornton is disavowing a trauma in his Irish past, for, unlike Paddy Bawn in Maurice Walsh's story or the early drafts of the film, he has no direct involvement in the War of Independence. It is, rather, as if the strong undercurrents of political violence in Walsh's story and Ford's own personal experience of the Black and Tans have been re-routed from the political domain of the Troubles into the personal trauma of Sean's American experience, while retaining the force of the original.

There is nothing unusual in resorting to *displacement* as an aesthetic device – or defence mechanism – for it figures as one of the primary means of screening off unwanted psychic material in Freud's analysis of dreams and the unconscious. What is at stake here, however, is *geographical* displacement, the projecting onto another territory or region of disturbing material from one's own national past – or present. The most obvious examples in recent cinema are, perhaps, the displacement of the turmoil and confusion of the Vietnam war onto the Old West in renegade westerns such as *The Wild Bunch* (dir. Sam Peckinpah, 1969), *Soldier Blue* (dir. Ralph Nelson, 1970*)*, *Little Big Man* (dir. Arthur Penn, 1970) or *Ulzana's Raid* (dir. Robert Aldrich, 1972) – though it could also be argued that part of the problem with the Vietnam war itself was the projection of the western onto the refractory 'wilderness' of East Asia. Ford himself was responsible for one of the pre-eminent examples of this kind of national allegory when in *Rio Grande* (1950), the film that first brought John Wayne and Maureen O'Hara together, the cavalry pursues the enemy across the border into Mexico, thus giving vent to the contemporary frustration of the American army at being unable to cross the 48th parallel. As General Sheridan says in the film: 'I want you to cross the Rio Grande, hit the Apache and burn them out; I'm tired of hit and run, I'm sick of diplomatic hide and seek.' *Rio Grande* also shares with *The Quiet Man* an attempt to bury the memory of a violent transgression in the past, in this case the burning down by Lieutenant-Colonel Kirby Yorke (John Wayne) of his wife Kathleen's (Maureen O'Hara) home during the Civil War. This gives a sardonic twist to the nostalgic Irish ballad, 'I'll Take You Home Again, Kathleen', which features in the film as it does on the soundtrack of *The Quiet Man*, and Yorke's ritualistic courting of his wife, carrying a bouquet of flowers to her quarters in the fort, also anticipates Sean's wooing of Mary Kate Danaher.

Faint echoes of 'the Troubles' and Ireland's violent political past nonetheless find their way into *The Quiet Man*, but often as seemingly throwaway remarks or cryptic asides that conceal more than they reveal. When Sean is first introduced to the worldly Father Peter Lonergan by Michaeleen Oge Flynn on the journey from the station, the priest replies with a classic sly understatement: 'Ah yes, I knew your people, Sean. Your grandfather, he died in Australia, in a penal colony. And your father, he was a good man too. Bad accident that.' This allusion to agrarian crime and deportation (no doubt for sheep-stealing, in keeping with its pastoral vision of the Irish countryside) is picked up in the hotel bar sequence when the locals, on hearing of Sean's ancestry, launch on cue into a rendition of 'The Wild Colonial Boy', a ballad about an Irish deportee who became 'a terror to Australia'. The action then cuts to an adjoining room of the hotel, where the IRA makes its appearance in the leisured guise of two characters who feature prominently in Walsh's *Green Rushes*, Hugh Forbes (Charles Fitzsimons [brother of Maureen O'Hara]) and Owen Glynn (Sean MacClory) – 'Sean Glynn' in the original. Dressed in the manner of Yeats's 'hard-riding country gentlemen', they act out to a risible degree the gentrified lifestyles of Walsh's characters but still elicit a salute from Michaeleen Oge when he enters the room:

MICHAELEEN OGE: Commandant Forbes!
FORBES: Ah, you can forget about the commandant, we're at peace now, man.
MICHAELEEN OGE: True, but I haven't given up hope.

Michaeleen's remark is virtually incomprehensible unless it is placed in the context of the original book and the earlier drafts, and the covert

Father Paul (James Lilburn) between takes

Mary Maguire and Bill Maguire (doubles for O'Hara and Wayne)

Martin Thornton, Maura Coyne and Jack MacGowran – watching the fight

Maureen O'Hara

Maura Coyne and the rest of the cast

Maureen O'Hara on set

John Ford directing the scene outside Curran's pub

Maureen O'Hara and John Wayne on set

allusions to the continuation of 'the struggle' are picked up when Michaeleen Oge walks Sean home to his cottage in the fading light and, holding his hand out to check the weather, remarks: 'Well, it's a nice soft night, so I think I'll join me comrades and talk a little treason.' Hugh Forbes and Owen Glynn make their next appearance even more incongruously as the organizers of the Innisfree races, and in what might be described as a 'Freudian sip' during Sean and Mary Kate's wedding ceremony, Forbes raises a glass to the couple: 'may they live in peace and [national] freedom.' On the recorded soundtrack the word 'national' is uttered, but it was crudely deleted in the final edit at the behest of Herbert Yates, the irascible head of Republic studios.[59] A similar elision takes place a few minutes later when Red Will discovers he has been deceived about his own marriage prospects. Not without a hint of bigotry belying his 'squireen' status, he accuses the Protestant vicar of lying – 'it's bad enough for you people' – and then Father Lonergan – 'but my own priest . . .' This was to be followed by: 'And worst of all, the Irish Republican Army,' but once more there is a silent edit in keeping with the muteness of the 'Quiet Man'.[60]

It is in the climactic harvesting sequence near the end, when Sean finally claims Mary Kate's right to her dowry off her boorish brother, Red Will, that the only menacing note is struck. Responding to Sean's demand for three hundred and fifty pounds, Red Will seems momentarily cornered when he notices that Hugh Forbes (still in jodhpurs) and Michaeleen Oge have also appeared on the scene:

> RED WILL: So the IRA is in this, eh?
> FORBES (*pointing to Red Will's house with his riding whip*): If it were, Red Will Danaher, not a scorched stone of your fine house would be left standing.
> MICHAELEEN OGE: A beautiful sentiment . . .

This is one of the few exchanges carried over directly from Walsh's story. When Paddy Bawn, with Ellen Roe in tow, challenges Red Will at the steam-driven threshing machine, he asks for a private word (as does Sean at an earlier point in the film), but Red Will is having none of it:

> 'Out with it! I don't care who hears.'
> He looked over Paddy Bawn's head at Mickeen Oge and Sean Glynn, his eyes fearless.
> 'Is the IRA in this too?' he enquired contemptuously.
> 'We are here as Paddy Bawn's friends,' said Sean [Glynn] mildly.
> 'The IRA is not in this, O'Danaher,' said Mickeen Oge, and he threw up his lean head and looked slowly towards the haggard. There was something in that bleak look that chilled even Red Will. 'If the IRA were in this, not even the desolation of desolation would be as desolate as Moyvalla,' that look seemed to say. (Walsh, p. 133)

The reference here is to the IRA campaign of burning 'Big Houses' in the 1920s, which were considered to be bastions of the Anglo-Irish Ascendancy. In *The Quiet Man*, however, it is not the Protestant community nor the Anglo-Irish who are the problem but the jumped-up rancher or 'squireen', Red Will. Such ranchers were also the target of IRA land agitation, and for Ford they signified the upper-class equivalent of the informer, the 'shoneen' who craves the lifestyle of his master and betrays the values of his own community. Ford's early expressionistic feature, *Hangman's House* (1928), his finest silent treatment of an Irish theme, ends with the burning of the hated castle of the 'Hanging Judge' O'Brien, the flames consuming the real villain of the piece, his informer son-in-law, John D'Arcy. The story turns on the resolve of a returned exile, Denis Hogan (Victor McLaglen), to seek justice for a primal transgression – D'Arcy's seduction and killing of his sister – and as the castle is going up in flames, the camera tilts downwards towards its reflection in the lake, in a Gothic premonition of the opening credit sequence featuring Ashford Castle in *The Quiet Man*.

Burning as retribution – or resolution – is a central theme running through *The Quiet Man*, being linked originally with the 'Hell' of Sean's exile in America. 'Saints preserve us,' asks Michaeleen Oge when he drives Sean from the station, 'what do they feed you Irishmen on in Pittsburgh?' 'Steel, Michael Oge,' Sean replies, 'steel and pig-iron furnaces so hot a man forgets his fear of Hell; when you're hard enough, tough enough, other things, other things, Michaeleen.' The 'other things' concern Sean's experience of Hell in the ring, but in the preliminary script notes this is linked in turn to the Troubles in Ireland through the mention of the blacksmith's furnace: 'A blacksmith taking off his apron, putting out the fire in his furnace, puts on his cap, and hastily ties up a bundle in which we can see three rifles . . .' This motif reappears in Frank Nugent's notes for the screenplay which stipulated that a furnace had to be in the background (along with the IRA) for Sean's final confrontation with Red Will: 'a machine or a gadget with a firebox in it; a harvester or blacksmith's forge'. But the searing heat of Sean's 'Hell' in America that the film seeks to exorcize may have a more direct relation to the Troubles, as we have seen, in Ford's own first-hand encounter with the burnt-out shell of the Thornton home, razed to the ground by the Black and Tans, during his visit to Ireland in 1921.[61] Sean's decisive act of throwing the cash he receives from Red Will for the dowry into the red-hot furnace of the harvester[62] – the door being opened by Mary Kate – may thus be seen as a narrative undoing of the displaced trauma of having killed a man in the hell of America for 'dirty money', a returning to the scene of the crime to purge it from memory. The ensuing protracted fight scene, parodically paying lip-service to the Marquess of Queensberry rules, follows through the logic of this re-enactment, as if Sean, like a witch's curse, has to go in reverse motion through the chain of events which brought him to the verge of breakdown in America.

Therapy on the Ropes

Ford manipulates antiquated structures . . . into contemporary liberal configurations. In other words, he works towards the future through the past (not unlike psychotherapy).

Brandon French, *On the Verge of Revolt*, 1977[63]

It is at this point that the horror of the darkest moment in the film – the traumatic flashback sequence when Red Will knocks Sean to the floor with a punch at the wedding ceremony – becomes apparent. For Martin Scorsese, as we have seen in the introduction, this flashback is the true precursor of the murderous fury unleashed in his film, *Raging Bull*, the garish colours highlighting its nightmarish qualities. In this short sequence, which lasts barely one minute, Scorsese is right to discern a whole narrative compressed to breaking-point. Ford's powerful use of the flashback is especially appropriate in this context of shock and concussion, given the intricate historical connections between the emergence of flashback techniques as a narrative device in cinema from 1914 onwards, and the simultaneous appearance of shell-shock or post-traumatic stress disorder as a clinical condition in World War I. Flashbacks of a rudimentary kind existed in cinema from the first experiments in editing as a means of reverting back in time, but it was not until *c.* 1910 that they were expressly linked to personal memory. One of the earliest uses of the flashback in this advanced sense occurs in Sidney Olcott's *The Lad from Old Ireland* (1910), often described as the first Irish feature film and, in many ways, the precursor of *The Quiet Man*.[64] Olcott's film deals with the theme of a returned emigrant, in this case Terry O'Connor (Sidney Olcott), who comes home from New York to save his sweetheart in Ireland, Aileene (Gene Gauntier), from eviction. On the journey back, Terry is shown on the open deck of the ship pining for his sweetheart, whose image suddenly appears beside him on the screen, superimposed on the original ocean setting. As if to say 'Hey, is this real?' he reaches

Plate 9.   Poster for The Lad from Old Ireland.

impulsively to grasp her but she immediately vanishes from sight. The action then cuts to the emigrant arriving at the country station, with a railway porter rather than a jarvey picking up his luggage. As Maureen Turim points out, such early flashbacks still have an indeterminate status, since, though they involve memory, they could also function as visions or hallucinations (not unlike the apparition of Mary Kate which first captivates Sean in *The Quiet Man*, and which prompts him to question its veracity).[65] It is not until flashbacks are clearly narrativized – for example, when they follow an intertitle or, later, a voice-over introducing a story in the past tense – that we can say that they are fully operating in the service of memory. This is the role of Father Lonergan's protracted voice-over, which frames the entire story of *The Quiet Man* – 'Well, then, now I'll begin at the beginning . . .' – though, as we shall see, this framing voice-over is not without its problems as a source of reliable narration.

The most vivid and arresting use of flashback, however, and the one that evokes most powerfully the experience of trauma, is that which disrupts narrative, as when a scene or sequence suddenly breaks into the action without any prior warning or motivation. This was indeed part of the new symptomatology of shock diagnosed for the first time among those whose minds were shattered by the mechanized ferocity of World War I. As Wendy Holden writes of the first appearance of shell-shock:

> Most of the symptoms witnessed during the First World War have been seen in veterans of every war since. Amnesia, nightmares and flashbacks are familiar today as indications of trauma. But faced with these manifestations in previously normal people for the first time, the medical staff of the 1914–18 war were baffled and, in many cases, overwhelmed.[66]

The term 'flashback' was not used at first for trauma – 'acute recollection' and similar terms were the norm – nor was it used in cinema: terms like 'switch-back', 'cutaway' and 'cut-back' vied for ascendancy until the word 'flashback' came into fashion. The crucial factor in both cases is the absence of any marker which locates the event firmly in the past as in, for example, the use of 'fades', 'dissolves', or a verbal past tense in voice-over: such is the painful immediacy of the experience that it seems to belong to the present. 'Pictures have no tense,' wrote the critic Bela Balazs in his pioneering *Theory of the Film*, 'they only show the present – they cannot express a past or a future tense.'[67] Flashbacks in the more manageable sense belong to voluntary memory, and lend themselves readily to a coherent narrative or, for that matter, to nostalgia. These are the dominant modes of narration in *The Quiet Man*, whether through Father Peter's overarching flashback, or 'the flashback-within-a-flashback' device, as when the voice of Sean's mother summons up an idyllic vision of his cottage that seems to belong more to the past than the present. Sean's reverie on this occasion may not be entirely voluntary, as it is triggered by a glimpse of his ancestral home: nostalgia of this kind is not too far removed from the involuntary flashes of trauma, except it has managed to screen off the pain of guilt and loss.

The first fully-fledged use of unmotivated flashbacks, cut adrift from visual mnemonic devices (fades, dissolves), voice-overs or narrative itself, is generally considered to be Alan Resnais's *Hiroshima Mon Amour* (1959), a disorienting and harrowing restaging of the long-term consequences of the trauma of World War II. Coinciding with Godard's innovation of the jump-cut in *Breathless* (1960), Resnais's flashbacks might more accurately be termed 'flash-cuts', due to the way abrupt, seemingly random memory traces of the Nazi occupation of France and Hiroshima intrude into the action.[68] Sean's flashback in *The Quiet Man* is of this variety, and is not unlike the first remarkable flash-cut in *Hiroshima Mon Amour*, which, though inexplicable at such an early point in the film, is nevertheless prompted by the visual rhyme between the hand of the Japanese lover of the (nameless) female protagonist and the hand of a dead German soldier, her former lover in a doomed, collaborationist romance. In *The Quiet Man*, Red Will's punch triggers a grim succession of scenes in flashback: Sean's opponent in the ring, spread-eagled on the ground in his blood-red shorts; the manic close-ups of Sean and his team staring like police suspects into the camera; the flashes of the press cameras simulating the flashback device itself; the doctor with his mournful black case; and finally the ritual of placing a towel over the dead boxer's face before we see Sean's anguished face in close-up. This flashback is all but unintelligible to the viewer at this stage, but in retrospect, certain narrative pointers can be deciphered. When the

Reverend Mr Playfair first hears Sean's name at his cottage, he mulls over it: 'Thornton . . . it has a familiar ring to it . . . ring to it . . . Thornton . . .' Mr Playfair is the only character who is in on Sean's secret throughout the film, but even he almost lets it slip when he seeks to restrain Sean from retaliating after Red Will has felled him: 'Steady, Trooper, steady. . .' By means of the dramatic force of the flashback, and later the more cumbersome device of Mr Playfair's scrapbook which traces 'Trooper Thorn's' fighting career, Sean's reticence to confront Red Will is belatedly explained. As in Maurice Walsh's original, the 'quietness' of the 'quiet man' is revealed not as meekness, nor as the absence of something to say, but as emotional excess and overload, the ominous silence of death.

It is at this point that one of the enigmas of the experience of trauma comes to the fore in a manner that underpins the silence and restraint of the 'Quiet Man'. If violence – or anything that recalled it – is such a source of stress to Sean throughout the film, why then does the action culminate in the violent spree of an interminable Donnybrook? The issue here has to do with *repetition*, or rather different modes of repetition, as a response to trauma: one, which is a (painful) continuation of an original event; the other, which introduces distancing of the kind that allows the sufferer to come to terms with the suffering. According to Susan J. Brison:

> Memories of traumatic events can be themselves traumatic: uncontrollable, intrusive, and frequently somatic. They are experienced by the survivor as inflicted, not chosen – as flashbacks to the events themselves. In contrast, narrating memories to others (who are strong enough and empathic enough to listen) empowers survivors to gain more control over the traces left by trauma. Narrative memory is not passively endured; rather, it is an act on the part of a narrator, a speech act that defuses traumatic memory . . . This is not to say that narrating one's memories of trauma is always

therapeutic, nor that it is, by itself, sufficient for recovery from trauma. But that such narratives contribute significantly to such is currently accepted as uncontroversial in the field of the psychology of trauma.[69]

As the sobriquet of the 'Quiet Man' indicates, however, the most notable aspect of Sean's 'recovery' in the film is that he does *not* tell his own story, but rather transfers his allegiances to a larger collective story – that of the imagined community of 'Innisfree' as refracted through that profoundly unreliable narrator, Father Peter Lonergan. It is thus not so much a talking as a social, theatrical cure, with its emphasis on ritual, custom and communal mores, that relieves Sean of the burden of his (American) past – if, that is, it can be considered a cure at all. The two confessional scenes that follow the breakdown in Sean and Mary Kate's marital relations are parodic to the point of being counter-confessional: Mary Kate's muffled confession in Irish to Father Peter simply distracts him from his fishing, while Sean confesses to the Reverend Mr Playfair only what the vicar knows already, and ends up hearing Mr Playfair's own confession about his far from brilliant boxing career. Sean's problem is not that of subsuming a discordant, random event into a more coherent personal narrative, for he seeks to repudiate his American experience rather than integrate it seamlessly into his life. Such is the grip of American national narratives on his past that Sean is looking for a way *out of*, rather than a way in to, narrative, and it is for this reason that the very disjunctions in the plot-structure of *The Quiet Man* serve to disrupt the kind of cohesion or closure endemic to Hollywood 'happy endings'.

From the outset, *The Quiet Man* contests the very basis of the talking cure or therapeutic narratives, the assumption that 'telling the story' is sufficient to integrate traumatic experiences into one's life. Not alone is Sean resistant to the talking cure, but those who have a lot to say, such as Michaeleen Oge, are hardly exemplars of straight-talking, or telling it as it is. Whereas the flash-cut to the death in the ring displays the force of a brute intrusion of reality into Sean's subjective world, the same can hardly be said for the unreliable, lackadaisical narration of Father Peter Lonergan, both in voice-over and flashback, which spans virtually the entire film. (The fact that Father Lonergan refers to himself as 'saintly-looking' indicates that this exercise in oral narration proceeds with the tongue firmly in the cheek.) 'Well, then, I'll begin at the beginning', he announces as the train bearing Sean draws into the station:

> FR LONERGAN (*in voice-over*): A fine soft day in the spring it was when the train pulled into Castletown, three hours late as usual, and himself got off. He didn't have the look of an American tourist at all about him, not a camera on him, and what was worse, not even a fishing rod.

We can establish from the images on the screen that this more or less accords with the facts, but the problem for the voice-over is that Father Lonergan was not there himself, and hence is in no position to act as eyewitness. It turns out, as we see a short time later, that he is some distance away in Innisfree, on one of his leisurely strolls through the countryside, and this introduces another twist in the tale. Though voice-overs, for the most part, indicate a flashback mode, Father Lonergan seems to be narrating events that are taking place in the present. As Michaeleen Oge's pony-trap with Sean on board comes into view in the green parkland, the voice-over picks up again: 'Now, then, here comes myself. That's me there walking, that tall saintly-looking man, Peter Lonergan, Parish Priest . . .' This may help to throw light on Father Lonergan's previous description of Sean's arrival at the station, for it is as if, in *Tristram Shandy* fashion, he is retrospectively watching the film itself, either in the cutting room or in the audience, thus drawing attention to its fictive status even as it unfolds before us on the screen.[70] From an external vantage point, Father Lonergan then moves to a position inside the story as

Michaeleen addresses him and introduces him to Sean. This anomalous 'post-production' commentary on what is taking place in the film seems to extend at times to the soundtrack as well. On discovering that Mary Kate has absconded to make her escape to Dublin, Sean saddles his horse, western-style, to ride to the rescue, leaving Michaeleen Oge on his hunkers, lilting to himself 'The Rakes of Mallow'. As if taking its cue from the wily matchmaker, the soundtrack then picks up the tune, giving it the full orchestral treatment.

The blurring of the boundaries between artifice and illusion, and Father Lonergan's oscillation between participant, spectator and narrator, is thrown into total disarray at the end of the film when the action appears to be drawing to a close. The Donnybrook having achieved its desired effect, Sean and Red Will stumble across another brook, arm-in-arm, singing the 'Wild Colonial Boy' on their way to White O'Morn. Mary Kate serves their dinner (as well as plying them with more drink), a ritualistic meal that provides the cue for Father Lonergan to wind up the Arcadian idyll: 'Well then, so peace and quiet came once again to Innisfree . . .' At this point, the story suddenly slips its narrative moorings as the tranquillity is disrupted by a shot of Mrs Playfair cycling on the tandem at breakneck pace to join a crowd on the bridge:

> FR LONERGAN: We were up . . . Good heavens!!! What's that woman up to now? [*Shouting*] Make way! Make way! She'll be running you down with that juggernaut!

The initial part of the narration, in the past tense, is outside the action, but the abrupt appearance of Mrs Playfair brings about an inexplicable transition to the present tense. As the camera follows Mrs Playfair, Father Lonergan comes into shot among the crowd, suggesting that the shouts of warning have been uttered by him on the bridge. 'In these shots,' Richard Neupert notes in his detailed analysis of the narrative structure of *The Quiet Man*, 'the text has moved from imminent closure in the form of a concluding comment by Lonergan and a static end image of Innisfree, to a re-opening of actions, underlined by Lonergan's own question, "What's that woman up to?" [71] Such are the narrative complexities, if not confusions, at this point that Neupert feels compelled, like those historians of early Irish Christianity who posited the existence of two St Patricks, to propose that there are two Father Lonergans: 'one is a character who is limited like all the others by the story's time and space; the second is a limited character-narrator who knows more than Lonergan the character, but less than the film's primary narrator'.[72] Though Father Lonergan's voice-over has apparently framed the action from the beginning, in effect he loses control of the narrative at the end, thus putting paid to any residual hope that the talking cure will bring about the necessary closure for the story.

In a more visceral sense than Father Lonergan, Sean also seems to be grappling with the competing claims of two lives, one in Ireland, the other in America. Sean is concerned to work through his tragic American past, but his method is not so much to get in touch with his feelings as with his community and his background. In fact, the community seems to come between him and his impulses, throwing all kinds of obstacles in the way of the direct methods that come so naturally to an individualistic pursuit of happiness. Redemption, if such there is, in Innisfree comes not through the word (which is almost perverted as soon as it is spoken) but through the deed, the re-enactments and rituals that invest everyday life itself with the symbolic force of language. Transplanted onto American ground, these rituals of family and community punctuate the White Anglo-Saxon and Protestant world of Ford's westerns with a sacramental reverence, or else with the collective abandon of the carnivalesque. Unlike its American counterpart, with its homage to Nature and the 'big empty', the myth of the West in Ireland is more concerned with what *overlays* nature, the accretions of culture and conflict deposited by history. If Ford shows an unusual sensitivity towards landscape –

whether it be that of Mayo or Monument Valley – it is because of his capacity to see in outdoor locations the expressive qualities of a studio set, while yet displaying all its imposing grandeur. *The Quiet Man*, as Lord Killanin claimed, may be an Irish western, but it is a western in reverse, a captivity narrative in which the victim is more than willing to be held captive by the natives and is prepared to fight for admission to the reservation.

3

'HEY, IS THAT REAL?': THE MIRAGE OF MEMORY

Tragedy no longer faces us as stark reality but is seen through the soft, coloured haze of sentiment either anticipatory or retrospective.
Erwin Panofsky, '*Et in Arcadia Ego*: Poussin and the Elegiac Tradition', 1955[73]

In Nicholas Poussin's famous painting *The Arcadian Shepherds* (1629–30), one of the great meditations on the paradise theme in Western art, a group of shepherds is shown contemplating a tomb in an Edenic setting bearing the inscription (presumably enunciated by Death): 'Et in Arcadia Ego' ('I, too, am in Arcadia'). Humanity, it seems, has no sooner discovered paradise than death invades its precincts, shattering the dream from the outset. Few more poignant images exist in Western culture of the fragility of the myth of the Golden Age, a land of perfection and bliss free from all the scourges of a fallen world: adversity, loss, suffering and, ultimately, death. In the earlier version of Poussin's painting, as Erwin Panofsky points out, the shepherds are startled and uncomprehending at the fatal disruption of their rural idyll: 'Death catches youth by the throat, so to speak, and "bids it remember the end".'[74] In the later, more familiar, version in the Louvre, however, the mood is altogether different and the shepherds are shown calmly brooding on their momentous discovery. The epitaph no longer seems to emanate from Death, or the tomb itself, but from its occupant, a shift which effects a subtle transition from the present to a more reassuring past tense: 'I, too, *was* once in Arcadia.' Shock is mellowed through hindsight, and the dream of Arcadia is retained through the elegiac tones of nostalgia:

Plate 10. Les Bergers d'Arcadie *(Nicolas Poussin).*

> Here, then, we have the occupant of the tomb substituted
> for the tomb itself, and the whole phrase projected into the
> past: what had been a menace has become a remembrance.[75]

In this we have something akin to the psychic journey of Sean
Thornton in *The Quiet Man*, though with important differences, as
we shall see. For all its effusive romanticism, death is never far from
the surface, giving even comedy itself a macabre touch. The sudden
intrusion of death into the levity of the wedding celebrations in *The
Quiet Man* – the frightening flashback sequence follows as a stark
contrast to a rollicking performance of 'The Humour Is On Me Now'
– shatters Sean's idyll of home, and from that moment on there is no
going back for him or, for that matter, the viewer. But while there is
no clear narrative anticipation of the flashback, as we have noted in
the previous chapter, this dark shadow does not fall entirely without
warning, and throughout the film scenes of comedy and intimacy are

67

frequently offset by ominous undertones of death. In the scene which immediately precedes the wedding, Sean and Mary Kate escape on a bicycle made for two from the attentions of Michaeleen Oge in his role of chaperone and matchmaker, only to end up embracing passionately in the graveyard – thus giving literal expression to that most amorous of traditional Irish marriage proposals: 'How would you like to be buried with my people?' As Brandon French describes this scene:

> As they kiss blissfully in that garden of death – an evocation of the original fall, which introduced death into the world – a thunderstorm suddenly erupts and drenches them, like God's wrath. Awed and chastened, they cling to one another, the passion of their initial embrace subdued.[76]

Death is also in some of the incidental cameos, as when Red Will's factotum Feeney (Jack MacGowran) moves Mary Kate's spinet into Sean's cottage, a candle placed at both ends, and intones as if carrying a coffin: 'God bless all here.' Death does not have the last laugh, however. In one of the final scenes, a set-piece borrowed from Dion Boucicault's nineteenth-century melodrama *The Shaughran*, an infirm Dan Tobin (played by Francis Ford, the director's brother) rises from his deathbed and can hardly wait to put on his trousers in his indecent haste as he rushes out the door to join the communal brawl at the end.

Ford himself spoke explicitly of his desire to 'discover humour in the midst of tragedy, for tragedy is never wholly tragic. Sometimes tragedy is ridiculous.'[77] The mock solemnity of an Irish wake lent itself to this fusion of the sublime and the ridiculous, and in this may lie an alternative mode of working through trauma to that of the confessional cure in a therapeutic culture. 'You can buy me a drink at your wake, ha, ha – and not before,' quips Red Will to Sean when they fight over who's paying for drink in the middle of their own fight. If the grim flashback sequence signifies the irruption of death into the Garden of Eden, Ford's film also allows for the ironic play on the 'Et in Arcadia Ego' theme elaborated by later artists who introduced lovers into the graveyard setting, as if to say: 'Even in death, there may be Arcady.' Instead of displaying solemnity, Irish wakes and keening customs were noted for their revelry, particularly with regard to storytelling, singing and dancing, and, most scandalously in the eyes of Victorian observers, drinking and bawdy sexual practices. Matchmaking was also carried on at wakes, which makes Sean and Mary Kate's tryst in a country churchyard seem less out of keeping with their own culture.[78] It is at that moment that Sean and Mary Kate decide to cut through the proprieties of courting and throw caution to the wind – at which point the heavens open in a thunderstorm as if the laws of nature have indeed been disturbed and custom has broken free from the dead weight of conservatism. Yet it would be mistaken to construe this as a rejection of tradition, the triumph of direct access to Nature and the body over the mediations of culture and history. This is the way Sean sees it at first, voicing sentiments that seem to belong more to the individualism of the cowboy in the western genre: 'I don't get this,' he complains when Michaeleen Oge assumes the role of chaperone to his courting of Mary Kate, 'Why do we have to have you along? Back in the States, I'd drive up, honk the horn, and a gal would come running.' This insensitivity to the social role of rituals ultimately comes between him and Mary Kate when his inability to understand the importance she attaches to her dowry leads to the breakdown in their marriage. For Sean it is one more custom cramping his style, another constraint on his American notions of freedom, whereas for Mary Kate it is the key to her freedom: 'Until I have my dowry safe about me,' she protests, 'I'm no married woman. I'm the servant I've always been – without anything of my own.'

Customs prevail in *The Quiet Man* but in the context of a modernizing society through which they retain their collective character but are no longer 'second nature', devoid of any critical or reflexive component. Sean Thornton is both native and stranger, a fast (or slow?) learner who does not imbibe tradition so much as work through it, even in the very act of questioning its authority. 'It's your custom, not mine,' he exclaims, handing Mary Kate back to Red Will by throwing her at his feet when he refuses to pay her dowry: 'No fortune, no marriage, we call it quits.' Sean brings with him individualist myths from his American upbringing, particularly having to do with freedom and choice in romantic love, but he is also in flight from the dark side of the American dream: the ruthless pursuit of profit and money at the expense of all other human and moral considerations. When he takes his troubles to Mr Playfair, the only one who knows about his American past, he admits that he did not defeat his opponent out of sporting prowess but out of a craven lust for money:

> I didn't go in there to out-box him, I went in there to beat
> his brains out, to drive him into the canvas, to murder him,
> and that's what I did, for what? A purse, a piece of the gate,
> lousy money.

That Sean has not put this mentality behind him is clear from his response to the dowry system and his persistence in considering it in terms of money alone. Mr Playfair explains to him that it is not just about money, but about custom: 'an old, old custom. The fortune means more to her than just money.' Sean has renounced the profit principle, but he is still incapable of seeing beyond the cash nexus. In Ford's universe, it is this enlargement of vision, the ability to negotiate even economics and commerce in terms other than money and profit, which constitutes what is left of moral value in a fallen world.

For all his celebration of the American way of life, Ford's films are characterized by a profound disquiet about money and its destructive impact on the cohesion of family and community. As Peter Lehmann has shown, even when characters such as Abraham Lincoln, in *Young Mr Lincoln* (1939), engage in business – in Lincoln's case, as a shopkeeper – there is still an anxiety about profiteering and making money. Time and again in the film, social and personal values triumph over crude financial ones in the extending of credit, or paying debts, especially in the case of those in need. This distaste for the corrosive effects of money on communal obligations extends to the sleazy banker, Gatewood (Berton Churchill), in *Stagecoach* (1939), whose moral standing is less than that of the prostitute Dallas (Claire Trevor) or the other outcasts in the film. It is again evident in the venal trader Futterman (Peter Mamakos) in *The Searchers* (1956), who is prepared to deal in death through gunrunning with the Comanche to make money. It does not follow from this that Ford had socialist or leftist sympathies; his affinities are more with agrarian populism or what Michael Lowy refers to as 'Romantic Anti-Capitalism', a critique of bourgeois society from the point of view of values that pre-dated rather than post-dated capitalism.[79] From this perspective, as Lehmann explains, it is not so much capitalism that is morally bereft as the evil individuals who exploit it for their own greedy ends:

> Ford's vision of capitalism has no place for profit. Ford's good shopkeepers literally give things away while his evil ones are incessantly and solely driven by profit. Or perhaps, to put it more accurately, Ford begrudgingly recognized the necessary function of profit in capitalism by displacing it onto unsavoury characters.[80]

As against Tag Gallagher's contrast between Stanley Kubrick and Ford – 'Kubrick applies placeboes to our consciences, showing us that evil, warped men cause evil; but Ford makes us uncomfortable, showing us that fine, noble people cause evil'[81] – Lehmann contends that there is nothing fine about any of Ford's characters who succumb to the lure of money: 'Ford's films relentlessly and almost obsessively represent the evils of capitalism as resulting solely from evil, one-dimensional men.'[82]

In fact, Sean Thornton represents a striking exception to this rule, a good man who finds himself enmeshed in a ruthless system that brings out the worst in everyone. In this sense, Sean's predicament is closer to historian Joseph Lee's characterization of nineteenth-century Ireland as a society whose evils resulted from the fact that many good people were caught up in a vicious system.[83] The aspect of this system that impinges most directly on *The Quiet Man* is the dowry, a feature of Irish marriage custom – and pre-modern European marriages – that dates from the earliest times. So far from being archaic, however, the dowry took on a new lease of life with the spread of the cash economy in post-Famine Ireland, and, as late as the 1940s, was still important enough to weigh heavily on the Irish government's decision not to intervene in the practice of building 'dower houses', or second houses, on family farms to encourage earlier marriages.[84] The dowry, as it evolved in the nineteenth century, was essentially a cash transaction where money was handed over by the father of the bride to the groom's father as compensation for the loss of resources – mainly land – incurred by both parents and siblings to enable one son to start a new family. As such, it was very much part of a patriarchal system, but, as Joseph Lee notes, it was also bound up with women's financial autonomy, as it was meant to compensate for the loss of female earning power due to the collapse of the 'cottage' textile industry in the early decades of the century. A woman's standing was measured by the size of her dowry, and to marry without a dowry, as in the case of Daniel O'Connell's wife Maire, was to be greatly diminished in the eyes of the community.[85]

According to James MacKillop, Sean's rejection of the dowry by destroying the money at the end is an outright repudiation of tradition: 'He does not accept Irish custom; he obliterates it.'[86] This is not quite accurate, for Sean does not reject tradition as such but its contamination by money, precisely the feature Mr Playfair and Mary Kate object to in the film. Sean dispenses with one part of tradition – not its time-honoured, but more recent, market additions – and embraces another strand through his engagement with communal ritual that leads to his confrontation with Red Will, allowing him to purge the sins of his American past. By the same token, though Mary Kate rejects the financial aspect of the dowry she does not turn on her back on tradition altogether but, in fact, seeks to re-connect with it through her 'things', the goods and chattels she insists in bringing with her to her new home: 'my mother's and my mother's before . . . there's three hundred years of happy dreaming in those things of mine – I want them, I want my dream.' There is indeed a quotient of dreaming in this wish, for the inheritance of goods did not descend along a matriarchal line, whether in an immediate pre-Famine or post-Famine economy. Mary Kate's sentiments here do not draw on a hidden undercurrent of Irish culture so much as graft onto tradition the newly emerging ideas of women's independence in the early 1950s. It is tempting, given the dichotomies available at the time, to construe her sense of self-worth in terms of a clash between the loveless matches of traditional arranged marriages and liberal ideals of choice extolled by Hollywood depictions of romantic love – and this is indeed as Sean sees it. But Mary Kate, for all her dreaming, resists the Hollywood fantasy as well, and is more interested in establishing a material basis and communal recognition for equality within marriage.

According to Virginia Wright Wexman, the Hollywood cult of romantic love culminates not in marriage but in a wedding; just in case they do not live happily ever after, 'romantic love after marriage need not be portrayed'.[87] The trappings of romantic love are evident during the courtship sequences in *The Quiet Man* in Sean and Mary Kate's impatience with communal control of their 'company keeping' and, above all, in their desire to escape the surveillance of their far-from-vigilant chaperone, Michaeleen Oge. In a perceptive aside, Joseph McBride and Michael Wilmington compare the tempest that erupts during their embrace in the graveyard to 'a *Wuthering Heights* storm',[88] but it is perhaps the 1939 Hollywood version of Emily Brontë's novel, with its classic evocation of romantic love that transcends all class and social barriers, that comes more readily to mind. In the film version, directed by William Wyler, the wildness of the Yorkshire moors, at one remove from society and worldly affairs, provides the appropriate setting for the passion of romantic love, equally cut off from the constraints of culture and society. When Cathy (Merle Oberon) first returns to *Wuthering Heights* as the wife of the conceited Edgar Linton (David Niven), she attempts to put Heathcliff (Laurence Olivier) in his place by disowning any previous familiarity between them. Edgar tries to ingratiate himself with his new wife by adding further snide comments on Heathcliff's uncouth ways, but only succeeds in drawing the pent-up fury of Cathy's suppressed love for Heathcliff upon himself. Cathy rushes to her bedroom and, in a frenzied discarding of the raiments of culture – what Edmund Burke famously referred to as the 'decent drapery of life' – pulls her hatpin violently out of her hat and tears off her finery before setting off through the fields in her bare feet, and Victorian 'me Jane' costume. On the rocky outcrop of Peniston crag, their romantic haven, Heathcliff is waiting for her, and they fall into each other's arms, free from the stifling constraints of society and history:

> CATHY: Heathcliff, make the world stop right here. Make everything stop and stand still, and never move again. Make the moors never change and you and I never change . . . This is me, standing on the hill with you, this is me forever . . .
> HEATHCLIFF: Cathy, you're not thinking of that other world now –
> CATHY: Smell the heather . . .

Sean and Mary Kate's escape from the all-seeing eye of Michaeleen Oge is a parody of this scene, down to Mary Kate's shedding of her stockings, her running in her bare feet and gambolling through the fields, and the removal of her hatpin and hat. As the couple take to the freedom of the open countryside in radiant sunshine, they seem at first to be following the Hollywood route of seeking refuge in

Nature, but, as McBride and Wilmington observe, the opposite turns out to be the case: 'The couple's momentary freedom is suddenly weighed down by the forces of tradition: castles and ruins loom out of the landscape.'[89] Instead of escaping from society, the runaway couple plunge into culture and history as their romantic elopement terminates in the graveyard in a ruined abbey, one of the powerful symbols of Ireland's cultural past. The presence of ruins frames their journey from the outset, for as Mary Kate draws Sean from his American (and Hollywood) ways into Irish protocols of courting they pass through a landscape annotated with history:[90]

(i)   the ancient cross in Castletown (in actuality, the Market Cross of Cong), described in Father Lonergan's voice-over in the original screenplay as 'the centuries old Celtic Cross which has stood unchanged through wars and rebellions';

(ii) the neo-Gothic entrance to Ashford Castle, a ruin as artificial as the Hollywood set they end up in;

(iii) Ross Emily Abbey, a fourteenth-century Franciscan monastery described by Michaeleen Oge with his usual reverence for facts as 'the ancestral home of the ancient Flynns; it was taken from us by . . . by . . . the Druids' (it was perhaps remarks like these which led James Agee to write in exasperation of Ford's humour in *Fort Apache* (1948) that 'there is enough comedy to make me wish Cromwell had done a more thorough job'[91]).

When Sean and Mary Kate on their tandem bicycle break free from Michaeleen Oge's history lessons, Sean stops at one point like a good tourist to admire the scenery, but Mary Kate is having none of it, drawing his attention instead to a counter-attraction off-camera. This turns out to be the source of Innisfree in its earlier poetic incarnation:

(iv) W. B. Yeats's home in the Norman tower at Thoor Ballylee.

As Mary Kate removes her stockings underneath the tower, fairy music ripples over the soundtrack as if to signal entry to a new, enchanted world, which ends in:

(v)   the graveyard in the ruined abbey, where they finally embrace.

Though ruins and the 'memory of the dead' in Irish culture testify to historical trauma and loss, they also embody hope and regeneration as in the emblematic image in nationalist iconography of a round tower framed by a sunburst, the symbol of a new dawn. As such, ruins belong to a radically different dramaturgy of death than the individual, psychological trauma experienced by Sean in the ring in America, and point towards an alternative, cultural way of working through grief and loss than individualistic narratives of romantic love. Notwithstanding the elision in the final cut of the overt political material contained in Maurice Walsh's published stories and the original screen treatments, this submerged historical dimension resurfaces in the *mise-en-scène* of *The Quiet Man*. In keeping with the melodramatic convention that subject matter repressed in the narrative re-enters through form, the submerged world of grief and loss manifests itself through image and music, displaced onto an overwrought theatrical or visual style. This 'overwrought' style is the source of what Tag Gallagher has described as both the 'documentary and Brechtian aspects' of *The Quiet Man*, its tendency to send itself up in the midst of pathos or while revelling in its authentic locations or ethnographic details.[92]

Romanticism without Illusions

Is it ever possible to watch those smiling, cheering faces, shot at you with the brazenness of Eisenstein's peasants . . . [and forget that] Ford is still an expressionist, and in The Quiet Man *emotions are not merely represented, but articulated . . .*

Tag Gallagher, *John Ford: the Man and His Films*, 1986[93]

The paradox of the 'return to nature' in *The Quiet Man* is that ruins are not the only eloquent reminders of the persistence of culture and history on the Irish landscape: the blatant unreality of the studio sets themselves add to the artifice, ruling out any question of an immediate rapport with Nature or scenery. This 'flaw' in the visual style of the film was a source of some concern to contemporary viewers, and particularly those who valued the film for its use of outdoor locations. According to Lindsay Anderson:

> Some scenes (particularly towards the beginning of the picture) have a distinctively rough-and-ready, first-take air about them. And production difficulties – largely, one imagines, occasioned by bad weather on location – have necessitated a number of studio inserts in exterior sequences which are particularly regrettable in a film which elsewhere gains so immensely from the freshness and vividness of its sense of reality.[94]

It is doubtful if these lapses in pictorial realism can be attributed solely to the vagaries of the Irish weather, if only because there are similar stylistic breaks in other Ford films of the period.[95] Notwithstanding the stunning outdoor locations of *The Searchers* (1956), for instance, stylized studio sets and heightened colours also disrupt the verisimilitude at acute stress-points in the action, most notably the lurid red colour which illuminates both the landscape and the homestead of Ethan's (John Wayne) brother Aaron (Walter Coy) when it is attacked by the Comanche. As in the traumatic flashback to the fatal prizefight in *The Quiet Man*, this massacre scene is introduced by an abrupt cut rather than the dissolves that signal scene changes elsewhere in the film. As Peter Stowell notes, the fact that it is immediately preceded by the famous mid-shot of a brooding Ethan staring across the flank of his horse against the backdrop of Monument Valley suggests that we are viewing the scene through his fearful imagination – a form of subjective realism or an 'almost realistic dream state' which, Stowell contends, 'was most effectively used in *The Quiet Man* where virtually the entire film (from the moment the cart passes under the train) is the playing out of Sean Thornton's dream of returning to Ireland'.[96]

The implication here is that it is not only the obvious studio sequences which are coloured by a subjective camera in *The Quiet Man* but also the much vaunted outdoor locations and natural scenery. This scenic photography earned the cinematographer, Winton C. Hoch, an Oscar, and also drew considerable praise from contemporary reviewers. In Ireland, the *Evening Herald* reviewer singled out the 'healthy naturalness' of the photography as being one of its main concessions to realism, and the *Irish Independent*, in a similar vein, noted that, while the 'exaggerations' of the plot strained credibility:

> There can be no quarrel with Ford's fine treatment of the scenery he found in the West. It is a lovely background, caught in soft shades of technicolour and as real as one could wish. The camera lingers on it lovingly, almost reluctant, one would imagine at times, to be getting on with the story.[97]

But not everyone was so impressed. The cantankerous Herbert Yates, head of Republic pictures, who had thrown so many obstacles in the way of the production, complained that 'Everything's all green. Tell the cameraman to take the green filter off'[98] – though for Ford's daughter Barbara in the cutting-room this was part of its attraction: 'The film is beautiful. We have received five day's work and it looks just like a fairyland. They really hit it on the head when they named it the Emerald Isle. I never believed any place could be so lovely.'[99] Though changes in perception dictate otherwise now, it is easy to forget that black-and-white film was associated with actuality and realism, being reserved mainly for newsreels, documentaries, war films, gangster films, etc., whereas three-component technicolour was considered more appropriate for romance and fantasy, as in cartoons, musicals, costume romances, comedies and westerns.[100] It is this use of colour, according to Tag Gallagher, that allowed Ford to filter the entire film through an expressionist sensibility of the kind that had previously required studio-based production in the black-and-white era of the 1920s and 1930s:

Equally expressionist is Ford's use of colour in his artful, closed-formed, painterly compositions [in *The Quiet Man*]. One might argue that in *The Rising of the Moon* (1956 [*sic*]), Ford's second made-in-Ireland film, the subtle black-and-white photos have a more 'realist' air and better serve to document Ireland's countryside; but we should beware of falling . . . into the illusion that 'realist' is innately superior to (or more truthful than) 'expressionist'. Three-strip dye transfer Technicolor was . . . generally used not for naturalism but for glorious artifice. The deep scarlet of the roses is one such example, the greenness of the fields another – Ford was actually accused of painting the fields.[101]

The extent to which the Irish countryside as portrayed in the film is filtered through Sean's romantic – and traumatized – imagination is evident in the scene at the beginning when, on the journey from the station, Sean alights from Michaeleen Oge's pony-trap and is first captivated by the sight of his family cottage, White O'Morn. While the shots of the cottage, bathed in sunlight and surrounded by greenery, are clearly outdoor locations, the sombre landscape behind Sean's position on the bridge, with mountains dominating the background, is flat, poorly-lit and so obviously a back-projection that one expects his shadow to fall upon it.[102] In a crucial sense, the artifice of the studio set frames the 'real' outdoor locations that follow, for, instead of yielding a perspicuous vision of pure nature, the landscape is mediated through a point of view shot, tinted by Sean's nostalgia for home. Though Michaeleen Oge states matter-of-factly that 'it is nothing but a wee humble cottage', language, in the form of his mother's words in voice-over, intercepts Sean's line of vision and subordinates even visual perception to memory and desire:

MOTHER (*in voice-over*): Don't you remember it, Seaneen, and how it was? The road led up past the chapel and it wound and wound. And there was the field where Dan

Tobin's bull chased you. It was a lovely little house Seaneen, and the roses – your father used to tease me about them but he was that fond of them too.

According to Peter Stowell, the recasting of the landscape of Innisfree through Sean's state of mind begins as soon as the pony-trap bringing him from the station disappears under the railway bridge, as if parting with modernity to enter a dream-world.[103] But the possibility that what we are viewing is already at one remove from reality is intimated at the railway station itself when, in a brilliant reflexive vignette, Sean's first view of the Innisfree – and Michaeleen's trap – is screened through a window in the waiting-room, a frame within a frame. According to this cinematic convention, the world which subsequently unfolds before Sean's eyes may not be so much a reflection of reality as a projection of desire, an emanation of the 'heat-oppressed' brain he brought with him from the furnaces of Pittsburgh.[104]

Windows of Desire

Squares of light are more interesting than the open sky. They make it look more human by reducing the sky, and then the whole sky grows out of that small space.
John McGahern, *That They May Face the Rising Sun*, 2002[105]

'In many of Ford's films', writes Charles Affron, 'the first statement of a visual "theme" already seems to be its own recapitulation',[106] and this is as true of the windows in *The Quiet Man* as it is of the doors that frame the action in *The Searchers*. (In fact, doors themselves often function as windows, as in the half-door characteristic of the thatched cottage which features so prominently in the set design.) Windows in classic Hollywood romances function as 'thresholds of feeling', at once drawing us closer to the object of desire as everything excluded from the frame pales by comparison, yet distancing us in the very act of viewing by placing another barrier between the spectator and the dream-world beyond the screen. As Douglas Sirk remarked of the silver screen itself, as well as the windows, mirrors and paintings which give glimpses of unattainable worlds of longing and loss in his own films:

> Everything, even life, is eventually taken away from you. You cannot feel, cannot touch the expression, you can only reach its reflection. If you try to grasp happiness itself, your fingers only meet a surface of glass, because happiness has no existence of its own . . .[107]

The most memorable example in Ford of the power of windows to evoke unattainable ideals – whether of memory or of desire – is in the Gothic sequence at the end of *Fort Apache*(1948), where Colonel Kirby York (John Wayne) looks out of a window recalling the heroism of his massacred comrades in the Seventh Cavalry. As the camera cuts to a reverse shot of the window from the outside, the ghostly reflections of the fallen are visible on the glass, passing silently into 'that other world'.

It is perhaps because of this barrier between desire and its fulfilment that Sean Thornton smashes a window with a shout on first entering his windswept cottage – an act that echoes Heathcliff's breaking of a window in *Wuthering Heights* to regain Cathy's love. Sean's violent gesture prompts Mary Kate's startled response to her own reflection in a mirror, another frame within a frame, and drives her into his arms in the tempestuous kiss in the doorway of the cottage, the threshold between inner and outer worlds. Rain streaming down the window of her upstairs bedroom distils Mary Kate's longing and disappointment later on when Sean is turned away as a prospective suitor by Red Will – a classic image of the domestic confinement of female desire in Hollywood family melodrama. (This scene recalls similar sequences in *How Green Was My Valley* in which

Angharad gazes wistfully through an upstairs window at her diffident lover, Mr Gruffydd.) Sean himself is shot against the backdrop of a magnificent stained-glass window in a church when he first attempts to make contact with Mary Kate at morning Mass, and this motif is recapitulated when the fugitive lovers finally embrace passionately in the graveyard, framed perfectly by the arch of a ruined Romanesque window. Located in open spaces but yet defining it, the vaulted window signifies release rather than confinement, a merging of the body – to adapt Walter Benjamin – with its historical setting. The fragmentation of the ruin itself bears witness to the loss and incompleteness that lies at the heart of desire, a quest for paradise in a landscape of loss and death.

As the window motif indicates, *The Quiet Man* is framed by Sean's nostalgic vision from the outset, much as in the earlier *How Green Was My Valley* when the older Huw's gaze out of the window at the beginning of the film gives way to the dissolves which announce the flashbacks to his childhood, 'a highly subjective, terribly coloured depiction of reality, one in which a child's emotions of remembering take precedence over crass facts'.[108] As with Sean's first sighting of White O'Morn, voices also mediate and inflect this vision:

> HUW: Memory . . . Who can say what is real and what is not? Can I believe my friends are all gone when their voices are glory in my ears? No. And I will stand to say no and no again, for they remain a living truth within my mind. There are no fences or hedges around time that is gone.

Indeed, there may be no fences or hedges around the past, but there might be a window frame. Though the film is not shot literally from Huw's point of view, Ford, as Tag Gallagher points out, uses an array of devices to indicate Huw's narrative intonation throughout, whether through actual point of view shots (which are sparingly used), flashbacks, or voice-overs, in addition to scenes in which Huw is the compositional focal point, or in which the expressionist *mise-en-scène* evokes his inner moods or feelings. It is this which contributes to the 'stagey outsideness' in which 'everything has been choreographed, the better to reflect Huw's notion of life as a ritual: everywhere, whether in church or at Bronwen's presentation, ritual is expressed as flowing geometric motions'.[109] By the same token, *The Quiet Man* is suffused with Sean's state of mind, even in scenes not shot literally from his point of view. When Mrs Playfair first sees Sean's cottage, she commends him for restoring it 'the way all Irish cottages should look – and so seldom do', before adding, in relation to the paintwork: 'And only an American would have thought of emerald green' – a remark that can hardly have helped Herbert Yates rant against the forty shades of green in the film. In this scene – and throughout the action – it is as if Innisfree is being created in Sean's image, and if there are opposing views, they come not from Father Lonergan's faltering voice-over but from Mary Kate and her resistance to his romantic vision. It is perhaps for this reason that in one of the most subjective sequences in the film Sean's first sighting of Mary Kate, the camera – seemingly against the logic of Sean's gaze – shows the Wild Irish Girl in a low-angle medium close-up, returning his look from outside his point of view (and smiling to herself in the process, in a look recapitulated at the end when she walks away from the thresher, having attained her heart's desire).[110] Mary Kate's longing gaze (whether through windows, or framed by buildings and walls) is more than a match for Sean's and, as we shall see, releases him in the end from the images of both Heaven and Hell which have held him captive.

Resistance through Rituals

Recapitulation may well provide the underlying narrative logic of *The Quiet Man*: history repeating itself as ritual in order to bring about its own undoing. If Sean's journey home is prompted by a wish to escape the steel-furnaces of Pittsburgh, it is fitting that on first crossing the threshold of his ancestral cottage he is greeted by a fire, set for him – 'by way of being a good Christian act' – by the neighbourly Mary Kate. It is not only the lousy money of the dowry, moreover, that is consumed by flames at the end. The 'good stick to beat the lovely lady' handed to Sean by an older woman as he drags Mary Kate through the fields is prefigured by a scene in which Sean returns home after the breakdown of their marriage has become public. Standing by the fire, Mary Kate, in Des MacHale's description, 'slowly and deliberately hands him a stick to beat her with, the traditional method of punishment in an errant Irish wife, but he throws it into the fire before sitting down without a word. This is of course just a gesture on Mary Kate's part, because she knows very well that he is not the sort of man to beat his wife with a stick.' Clearly the local woman who hands Sean the stick later did not have such a high opinion of him, but MacHale is inclined to extend his benign reading of Sean's character (who, after all, has killed a man in the ring) to Irish males in general, particularly in relation to the controversial question of the role of domestic violence in the film:

> Local people, the Irish in general and Irish-Americans took the treatment of Mary Kate at face value and interpreted it in terms of brutality, wife-beating and the social humiliation of a woman. Many people in Galway and Mayo felt it had brought the West of Ireland into disrepute, and even today many people worldwide find it unacceptable. Of course such physical treatment of women never took place in the West of Ireland, at least not since caveman times and maybe not even then.[111]

In fact, just as Ford did not flinch from incorporating the physical violence associated with death in the ring into the film, by the same token the shameful secret of domestic violence is also brought into the open in the idyllic world of Innisfree.

That Ford was aware of the unerside of domestic life beneath the official ideals of faith and fatherland is clear from one of the books he sent to scriptwriter Frank Nugent for his research on the screenplay, Conrad Arensberg and Solon T. Kimball's classic anthropological study, *Family and Community in Ireland* (1940). Discussing responses in the Irish countryside to childless, if not unconsummated, marriages, Arensberg and Kimball note that 'the husband has every right to express his displeasure at his wife's barrenness . . . In the country districts they say he may beat her and in their graphic phrase "bounce a boot off her now and then for it".'[112] (One has only to look at the thatched cottage in the frontispiece of Arensberg and Kimball's book, moreover, with a more modern slated cottage cropped in the corner of the photograph, to see the prototype of White O'Morn.) As with the film's depiction of the dowry system, however, the important question is not so much its inclusion (as if this by itself is an endorsement), or even its sociological accuracy, as the narrative purpose it serves in Ford's film.

Plate 11. John Ford in Ireland.

More than any other aspect of the film, the curtain call at the end in which characters take their bow, or directly address the camera, calls attention to the theatricality of the action, and its resistance to Hollywood conventions of realism.[113] Not least of the ironies of this tableau seemingly tacked on at the end is that it also serves to undermine one of the classic forms of closure in Hollywood cinema, the reassuring entry into the 'real' world which follows a narrative sustained by the subjective flow of a voice-over, or flashbacks. As we have seen in Chapter 2, the promise of an idyllic ending as Father Lonergan's framing voice-over draws to a close is disrupted by a sudden intrusion of a 'reality' outside his narrative control – and which, indeed, renders problematic the position from which his flashback was narrated in the first place.[114] Again, as we have observed in Chapter 2, this shift in narration poses endless problems for locating where precisely Father Lonergan is speaking from, but nonetheless the epilogue seems to restore a 'real' world, and a sense of an integrated community, which brings the film to a satisfactory close. But is it a real world? And is it an authentic community? What we see is in fact a charade, a self-conscious simulation of a unified community to deceive the visiting Protestant bishop into thinking that the Reverend Mr Playfair still has a viable Protestant congregation, or at least the whole-hearted support of the community. Even Father Lonergan, true to his narrative dissembling, covers his priest's collar to pass himself off as a Protestant. The self-consciousness of this masquerade is taken a stage further in the closing cameos when the semblance of presenting a unified community to one outsider (the visiting Protestant bishop) is followed by a theatrical 'curtain-call' in which leading members of the cast (including one mystery character alongside the actor Jack MacGowran) take a bow or wave directly to the audience, as if to remind us both of the presence of the camera and the fact that we too are in the position of the bishop, viewing a mere pretence, a *representation* of community. According to Richard Neupert, some of these ambiguities may be resolved if we understand the characters/actors as addressing the camera from an indefinable space outside the action, but this is not so: they are clearly meant to be on the bridge, as indicated by the continuous parapet in the background. Compositional space and logic is broken in the final shot, however, in which Sean and Mary Kate wave to the audience. Though 'included within the circle of waving and looking' to establish their integration into the rest of the imaginary community, they are located in front of White O'Morn, some distance from Castletown. There is, however, a narrative logic to this parting shot, for, in a delightful aside, Mary Kate whispers something in Sean's ear, a physical re-enactment of his first view of White O'Morn during which a woman's voice – his mother's – also framed his vision. Sean immediately responds by throwing away 'the stick to beat the lovely lady' handed to him earlier, thus overtly rejecting this aspect of the traditional society he has married into. For many commentators, the enigma of Mary Kate's quiet word in Sean's ear has taken on something of the mystery of the Third Secret of Fatima, but one audacious interpretation suggests that she is, in effect, telling him that their revels are ended and that they need no longer keep up the pretence of marital discord. The implication here – given credence by both Des MacHale and Joseph McBride in their extensive discussions of the film – is that the entire sequence beginning with Sean dragging Mary Kate back from the station has been stage-managed to deceive Red Will into parting with his fortune to save face in the eyes of the community. As MacHale describes it:

> There has already been a major conspiracy in *The Quiet Man* so it is no surprise that [this] involves another conspiracy – this time between Mary Kate and Sean to force Danaher's hand and shame him into paying the dowry. This seems to be the way Ford directed it and Maureen O'Hara, who should know, told me in a personal interview that this is the way that she and the Duke were told to play it as the movie was being shot. If this is the case, then it changes everything

– *The Quiet Man* is not anti-woman, the drag across the field is all a sham, a comic caper, and Mary Kate, far from being abused, is merely going along with the act towards her personal triumph.[115]

This may be the key to the apparent anomaly identified by Brandon French in *The Quiet Man* in which a primal act of violence is simply repeated rather than purged on Sean's return to Ireland: 'The pivotal incompatibility of *The Quiet Man*'s plot is that Mary Kate's innocent desire to acquire her dowry requires Sean to duplicate the sin that caused his fall: the acquisition of money through violence.'[116] On this reading, the entire film would be an extension of the harrowing flashback sequence, in that traumatic repetition refuses any distance between past and present and produces simply a re-occurrence or re-opening of the original wound. The layers of mediation, however, which Ford introduces into the film – whether through narrative structures, framing devices, artificial set-ups or masquerade – places sufficient distance between the re-enactments and the originals to imbue them with the collective agency of rituals, if not quite the narrative closure of the talking cure. The past may not be purged, but at least it is no longer in a position to invade and overpower the present. If the traumatic past is kept at bay, other versions of restoring the past in all its plenitude are also rendered illusory, and not least the return to home. As Richard Neupert observes, though Sean may return to his home at the end of the film, it is a home divested of romantic illusions:

When Mary Kate whispers into Sean's ear, pulls away the ever-present stick, and leads him merrily back to the cabin . . . [t]he termination point is complete in that the fictional world's logic has been threatened by the direct address to the camera, hence Innisfree itself cannot be returned to.[117]

The film can thus be seen as a gradual disenchantment of Sean's nostalgic vision while yet allowing him to come to terms with the nightmare of his past. Mary Kate, literally, has the last word, a wake-up call releasing Sean from the dream of a return to paradise – 'another name for Heaven' – which was itself a product of trauma, death and loss, stoked by the furnaces of Pittsburgh 'so hot a man forgets his fear of Hell'. If there is redress for the injuries of his American experience, it comes through the community in the form of voice of 'the other' – which, as befits a 'Quiet Man', is more a listening than a talking cure.

Plate 12. '*Céad Míle Fáilte*'.

CONCLUSION

The Quiet Man *is not so much a sentimental film as a film about how*
such sentimentality operates . . . Mystification in Ford tends to be
accompanied by demystification: plenitude disappears even as it inscribed.
Paul Giles, 'The Cinema of Catholicism: John Ford and Robert
Altman', 1991[118]

The Quiet Man can justly lay claim to be the film that launched a
thousand ships – and planes – in search of its imaginary Ireland, as it
became virtually a master narrative in Bord Fáilte's (Irish Tourist
Board) promotion of Ireland abroad, especially for the American
market. Ford, as we have seen, had self-consciously exploited its
potential as a travelogue and, as Stephanie Rains has noted, Irish
travelogue films took him at his word in the 1950s and began to
incorporate fictional narratives of emigrants returning to the
homeland into their catalogues of scenic attractions.[119] One such film
is *O'Hara's Holiday* (1959), which not only trades on the star-appeal
of Maureen O'Hara in its title but depicts a New York policeman
visiting Ireland for the first time and falling in love with a Mary Kate
look-a-like, of the kind that was still in vogue when *National
Geographic* magazine visited Ireland in 1961 (with, appropriately,
Ashford Castle in the background) (Plate 13). Proving that the luck
of the Irish also comes with the full tourist package, O'Hara discovers
his Irish family and ancestral village by chance on his way back to
Shannon for the return flight.

Even closer to Ford's film is the idiosyncratic *The Spell of Ireland* (dir.
Danny Devlin, 1959) which veers between a disjointed geographical
tour, an anthropology lesson and, at a climactic narrative moment, an
imaginative out-take from Sean Thornton's first sight of Innisfree.[120]

The film is narrated in voice-over and takes the viewer – and prospective sightseer – initially on a jaunty round of familiar beauty spots and highlights of the social calendar such as the Gaelic football finals, the Galway Races and the Dublin Horse Show. No sooner has the tourist been presented with images of Ireland as a recreational paradise than the mood darkens and, as if to atone for previous pleasures, the viewer is brought on a harrowing pilgrimage in drastic weather up the side of Croagh Patrick in County Mayo. The previous narrative is derailed in what turns out to be a sombre anthropological digression, showing aged pilgrims braving it up the rocky mountainside in their bare feet in the dark. Various ambulance stations are pointed out, and the rigours of the 'penitential exercises' are intensified by a torrential storm of rain and sleet, culminating in scenes showing a mother and a baby being rescued and others being carted off on stretchers. Though hardly the Tourist's Board's idea of how to attract people to savour the delights of Ireland, an earlier excursus in the film showing the hardships of life on the Aran Islands relates these episodes to the 'hard primitivism' (in Erwin Panofsky's phrase) of Robert Flaherty's poetic documentary *Man of Aran* (1934), and, perhaps, the picturesque exoticism of *National Geographic* magazine (for which Croagh Patrick was a shrine to peasant superstition and piety).[121]

It is when the travelogue arrives in Donegal that the hitherto anonymous narrator himself loses the plot and takes a trip down memory lane. As the camera pans over a distant village in the manner of Sean's early point of view shot of Clifden from the bridge in *The Quiet Man*, it alights on a thatched cottage, activating a voice-over from the narrator's mother which suddenly intrudes on the soundtrack:

> MOTHER (*in voice-over*): Ah, yes, Seaneen, you've been gone a long time but your roots are still in Ireland. You were born in that little cottage, and it was your sister who kept the farm going for all you wains. And there was Rose, who helped to keep the family fed . . .

Plate 13. National Geographic, *March 1961. (A Maureen O'Hara lookalike, complete with Ashford Castle, location site for* The Quiet Man, *in the background.*

The voice-over then recalls various members of the family, who are no sooner named than they appear on the screen, sometimes looking directly at the camera. The technique here is not unlike Father Lonergan's flashback in *The Quiet Man* and, as if on cue, a scene with a young girl and a sheep in a green landscape appears – except that this time round, in an infantile counter-pastoral, she is a small child playing with her pet sheep:

> *Shot of small child,* MAGGIE, *playing – in fact, manhandling – a sheep.*
> MOTHER (*continuing in voice-over*): Will you ever forget the day when Maggie's pet sheep took a notion to be bold . . .
> *As* MAGGIE *attempts to walk away from the unruly sheep, it butts her on the behind, knocking her face forward onto the ground.*
> MOTHER: . . . but Maggie was well able for him . . .
> *The child lifts herself up and proceeds to kick the startled sheep repeatedly.*

Sean Thornton would have even more reason to ask 'Hey, is this real?' if Mary Kate, Mel Brooks fashion, took to kicking the sheep in her vicinity. The Irish equivalent of flogging a dead horse – or rather donkey – is seen in the next sequence as the mother recalls her son's playful participation as a child in 'a donkey elimination contest' or 'donkey derby' – an unwitting exposé of thoughtless cruelty to animals as young boys play musical chairs on donkeys, in some cases beating them to the ground. These are followed by flashbacks to the narrator himself as a young man footing the turf on the bog, and an elegiac tone enters as several of those named are described as having emigrated to England or America. The flashback ends with his mother's words, 'Ah, Seaneen, those were the happy, carefree days in Ireland,' before normal reception is restored and the narrative adjusts to its previous 'objective' travelogue format.[122]

The obvious question that arises here, as it does in relation to Ford's film, is: what were contemporary viewers to make of this? The fact that a pastiche of *The Quiet Man*'s most subjective sequences passed over unalloyed into the documentary/travelogue format suggests that romanticism had fused with realism, and that viewers were expected to take unbridled fantasy as possessing the same truth value as the reverential treatment of Croagh Patrick. Yet one hardly needed to be a film theorist to note the sheer incongruity between the narrative styles, and the implausibility of the flashbacks as documentary inserts. (Are we genuinely expected to believe that colour footage existed of the narrator's family from twenty or thirty years earlier? And that the mother is narrating, Father Lonergan fashion, from a studio, while watching the imaginary home movie?) The narrative discrepancies of *The Quiet Man* may not have been as blatant as *The Spell of Ireland*, but some reviewers, as we have seen, complained about the falsity of the sets and artificiality of the studio sequences, while others lavished praise on the natural outdoor locations and the vivid realization of the Irish countryside. This ambivalence passed over into responses to the stereotypical characters in the film, as in Donald Connery's observation in his book *The Irish* – one of the better journalistic attempts to update images of Ireland in the 1960s – that 'The popular image of the natives is a kind of gummy Irish stew of comedians, colleens, characters out of *The Quiet Man*, drunk poets, IRA gunmen, censorious priests and cantankerous old farmers who sleep with their boots on.' But, in keeping with the blurring of the boundaries between fact and fiction, Connery then proceeds to register his real complaint:

> The trouble is that every time I am solemnly told in Ireland that the stage Irishman does not exist I meet one the next day. There may not be a brogue (which is something I have heard only in New York) but the general behaviour – the torrent of words, the jokes, the devil-may-care jauntiness and the great fondness for alcohol – is enough to confirm every stereotype.[123]

Connery is drawing attention here to an important though often neglected aspect of stereotypes: that instead of being misrepresentations, they may represent reality all too well – and therein lies the problem. The most difficult stereotypes to uproot are not those that falsify reality but those that are grounded in truth, and which also go one step further in purporting to show the 'essence' of things: not only how things are, as matter of fact, but how they are in the order of things. Thus – to shift to a different set of examples – the difficulty with gender representations in children's school-books depicting Mam slaving over a hot stove and washing the clothes while Dad goes to work and washes the car, is not that they are untrue, but that they are portrayed as the norm, conveying essential truths about gender and sexuality. By the same token, ethnic markers or cultural differences, often accurate for the most part, calcify into stereotypes when they are cast as aspects of 'national character', or attributed to racial characteristics.

The task of challenging or combating a stereotype, then, is not simply a matter of showing the reality behind the myth but the reality *of* the myth, and the dynamics of its construction. '*The Quiet Man*,' as Paul Giles acutely observes, 'is not so much a sentimental film as a film about how such sentimentality operates.'[124] This involves a critical exposition of precisely the generic conventions of the myth which are taken as 'second nature' but which, in fact, have to be continually remade and renewed in the face of changing social and cultural circumstances. In this respect, John Ford's *The Searchers* may have contributed as much to the gradual de-mythologizing of the western genre as any amount of documentaries or social histories attending to the 'real facts', for it deconstructs the genre itself, unmasking the racism and civil savagery that underpinned the expansion of the American west and the freedom of the frontier. Films that effect paradigm shifts in this manner often seem to come before their time, or at least before the emergence of the manifold creative and critical responses that contribute to their becoming classics. *The Searchers* had, perhaps, to await the crisis of the Vietnam western for the full measure of its questioning of the American dream to become apparent. To ask whether audiences at the time of release were aware of these complexities is to miss the point: film classics of this kind become, in effect, genres in themselves, provoking new readings as they inspire other remakes, imitations or parodies. Whether in the form of modern captivity narratives such as *Taxi Driver* (dir. Martin Scorsese, 1976), *Hardcore* (dir. Paul Schrader, 1978) or *Dances With Wolves* (dir. Kevin Costner, 1990), or postmodern homages such as *Paris, Texas* (dir. Wim Wenders, 1984), *The Searchers* has been replayed time and again on the American screen.[125]

In a similar manner, the pervasive influence of *The Quiet Man* in Irish culture has passed over not only into postcards, tourist images and Irish-American nostalgia, but also into a sub-genre of 'therapeutic narratives' in Irish cinema. In these narratives, the romantic appeal of the Irish countryside and the search for home is offset against the disenchantment of life in the metropolis, but more specifically against traumas from the past for which modernity has no answer.[126] If the casting of tradition in terms of maternal attachment presides over *The Quiet Man*, then the obverse also holds and the sacrificial death of the mother is required for progress, as if modernization can only take place over her dead body. This is literally the case in Jim Sheridan's version of *The Field* (1990), where the Bull McCabe's obsession with his plot of land, and his implacable resistance to the modernizing designs of the visiting American, is traced eventually to the fact that his mother died (or, rather, was let die by the Bull and his father) in the field, so that her blood is commingled with the soil. This is not the only trauma the Bull McCabe is trying to escape from: he is also responsible for the death of his son Seamie by suicide. This gives rise to the phenomenon of the 'Quiet Woman' – as a result of his role in their son's death, the Bull's wife has not spoken to him for twenty years. The Bull McCabe is a more menacing, tragic counterpart to Red Will in Ford's film, the local farmer, complete with factotum (John Hurt), whose designs on the land are thwarted initially by an Anglo-Irish widow (Frances Tomelty) and then by a returned American (Tom Berenger). The flame-haired Wild Irish Girl (Jenny Conroy) also appears, but, as a member of the nomadic Traveller community, she represents a threat to the stability of the family farm and the courtship rituals of marriage. Unlike Sean Thornton, moreover, the returned 'Yank' is a more destructive, intrusive presence, subscribing to the industrial logic and profit motive rejected by Sean: instead of seeking to reconnect with the maternal past, his plan is to bury it forever under the concrete of a hydroelectric station. The Bull is closer to Sean Thornton's sentiments in pitting emotional and historical investment in the land against crude economic conceptions of modernization, but, in what can only be seen as a direct strike against cultural tourism and the growth of Irish-American interest in 'roots' and genealogy, the Bull lashes out at this sentimental Irish-American investment, contending that it was the diaspora who betrayed their ancestors at home by fleeing the country in their hour of need. Thus, the Bull batters the semi-concussed American to death on a rock while he berates the cowardice of the Irish-American diaspora:

> BULL (*out loud*): His family lived around here but when the going got tough, they ran away to America, they ran away from the famine, while we stayed – do you understand me, we stayed, WE STAYED . . . Go home, Yank . . . You went away to America to make a few dollars. Do you think you can come back here with those few dollars, and buy the land that you deserted?

The Field has a much less benign view of the encounter between progress and the past than *The Quiet Man*, but for all its harsh realism it may be more romantic in the end in its tragic rejection of modernity. In the Bull McCabe's universe, the occupier of the land seems to precede and, indeed, oppose the logic of capital, though, in truth, the type of ownership he claims makes no sense other than in terms of private property and agrarian capitalism. In *The Quiet Man*, by contrast, 'archaic' social customs such as the dowry are shown to be integrated into the cash economy – which is, indeed, why both Sean and Mary Kate repudiate this aspect of 'tradition' in the end.

In Paul Quinn's *This Is My Father* (1998), the returned American is Kieran Johnston (James Caan), a high-school teacher in Aurora, Illinois, facing a mid-life crisis due to burnout in his run-down inner-city school. It is significant that Kieran is a history teacher, and that the apathy and delinquency of his pupils in his multi-racial school stem in part from the historical void in their lives, and their inability to relate to their own communities and their pasts. The classroom scene opens with a teenage girl giving a botched version of her family tree, tracing it back to King Slovik of Norway and Eric the Red. This lack of rootedness is also Kieran's predicament, for it is as if the historical events that have shaped his life – and particularly the silence over his missing father – have never been raised to consciousness, which may itself have contributed to his loss of purpose and depression when the story opens. A chance discovery of a photograph of his mother before she emigrated from Ireland in 1939, with a handsome young man who turns out to be his father, acts as the catalyst which brings the disillusioned history teacher and his young nephew Jack (Jacob Tierney), a gauche teenager, to Ireland. As in the case of *The Quiet Man*, Kieran returns to the ruin of his ancestral cottage but the story that unravels about his parents' troubled relationship – narrated in flashback by an old Traveller woman (Moira Deady) – places the trauma at the heart of the story firmly on home ground. Kieran's father, Kieran O'Day (Aidan Quinn), turns out to have been an orphan, or 'poorhouse bastard', fostered to a local couple to help them on the farm, and it is this class background which blights his relationship with Kieran Johnston's mother, Fiona Flynn

(Moya Farrelly), the vivacious and rebellious daughter of a spiteful, well-off widow. The sullen opposition of the community, spearheaded by both church (the parish priest) and state (the police), to the doomed relationship comes to a head during a country dance when some local ne'er-do-wells spike Kieran's drink, leading to a vicious Donnybrook in the hall. As if taking a lead from *The Spell of Ireland*, the miserly parish priest (Eamonn Morrisey) launches a tirade from the pulpit next morning at Mass against lax moral standards in the community, and orders the entire parish to undertake a pilgrimage to nearby Croagh Patrick in penance. Kieran and Fiona's relationship begins in earnest when they manage to skive off from the pilgrimage and spend the day at a windswept beach, the occasion, it transpires, on which the photograph is taken that triggers Kieran Johnston's quest for home (the snapshot is taken by a globetrotting American photojournalist who happens to land his plane nearby – a *deus ex machina*, if ever there was one). To prevent Kieran winning her daughter's heart (and gaining her land), the Widow Flynn (Gina Moxley) threatens to evict his foster parents and forces Fiona out of her home to take the emigrant boat, thereby precipitating the crisis which leads the ill-fated Kieran to take his own life out of remorse for the damage he has inflicted on those closest to him.

If, as Martin McLoone remarks, the uninhibited Fiona Flynn 'is potentially a more liberated and liberating "feisty colleen" than Mary Kate in *The Quiet Man*', this is one of many ways in which *This Is My Father* acts as an ironic rejoinder to Ford's film.[127] Renouncing the myth of the West, it is in fact set in the decidedly unpicturesque Irish midlands, where two giant smokestacks of a turf-burning power station dominate the horizon. 'We've landed in Chernobyl,' exclaims Kieran Johnston's nephew Jack, as if he has hit on another name for hell. The version of the rural past which the film evokes is in keeping with this bleak vision, at least where the fortunes of Kieran O'Day are concerned. When Kieran first appears on the screen, he is singing 'The Wild Colonial Boy' as he herds cattle through a field screened

Plate 14. Fiona Flynn (Moya Farrelly).

by foliage, but in contrast to *The Quiet Man* it is the woman, Fiona, who is the viewer rather than the viewed as, dappled by sunlight, she proposes that Kieran bring her to the ill-fated dance that night. Much is made of 'the tinker's curse' inflicted on the Widow Flynn in bringing about his downfall, but it is clear that this has more to do with the stifling social conditions that prevailed for someone of his background in the countryside – in effect, a moral outcast within his own community. Though the film ends on a therapeutic note – the missing narrative behind the enigmatic photo is gradually put in place – this is not quite the talking cure of popular American psychology. As Jane M. Shattuc writes of the 'talk-show therapy' of confessional television shows such as *Oprah*, these are characterized by the vindication of a 'self-help' ethic as if both cause and cure operate entirely within the personal realm:

> Talk-show therapy is at best 'band-aid' therapy . . . Its logic downplays environmental factors or an awareness of what might be described as social subjectivity . . . The individual is so caught up in self-examination and self-determination that he or she denies any larger social causation. Depression has its social roots, yet it is denied here . . . [In the case of one programme in which a] couple lives in a trailer park and the unfaithful husband cannot find full-time work, the programme avoids discussion of possible economic determinants of the problem.[128]

Not least of the ironies of *This Is My Father* is that the veil thrown over the past has led Fiona herself, as an old woman on her deathbed in Illinois, to spend the time in a semi-comatose state viewing such talk shows, as if they compensate for the silence. The talkshow on afternoon television when we first see her features a raucous disagreement over paternity, suggesting that the travails of Ireland in the 1930s are not by any means over in America, especially among the social underclass that provides the bulk of Kieran's classroom. When he reads out the statistics indicating the grim prospects that lie before his pupils on their leaving school, the ineptness of talk-show therapy to deal with the scale of their problems is starkly evident.

The same can be said of the therapeutic narrative of *This Is My Father*, and it is striking that even though there is a happy ending of sorts, it signally fails to atone for the futility of Kieran O'Day's suicide. Such resolution as there is comes from a recognition that what presented itself to Kieran O'Day as a source of despair – the array of class, religious and social prejudices which passed for custom – is amenable to change, albeit over several decades, and this lesson is not lost on his son when he returns to his teaching post in America. The final scene in the film shows Kieran Johnston, the history teacher, appearing to gain the respect of his once disaffected class by passing around the photograph which sparked off the story –

presumably after he has related it to them. The implication here seems to be that even the deepest personal crises call for a reconnection with, and a renegotiation of, one's own ethnic and social background, all the more so if there is a need to change it. Unlike *Angela's Ashes* (dir. Alan Parker, 1999), Kieran does not simply reverse *The Quiet Man* by looking to America as the answer to Ireland's ills, but draws on his newly discovered, and far from romantic, Irish inheritance as a way of enabling others – the Kieran O'Days of Aurora, Illinois – to look at their own predicaments from the multiple perspectives of their own cultural pasts.

In *This Is My Father*, hearing the story and piecing together the shards of memory brings the narrative to a close, but *The Quiet Man*, as we have seen, goes beyond this. Here the 'hyphenated American' (to use Woodrow Wilson's phrase) does more than listen to stories and actually participates in a culture at once strange and familiar, taking its rituals and customs seriously – but not as second nature. The rituals of the dowry are undergone only to change them, and the throwing away of 'the stick to beat the lovely lady' gestures towards the end of the social order which brought Kieran O'Day to his doom. In this we see perhaps what might be described as a theatrical, as opposed to a therapeutic, culture in which re-enactment and repetition bring a mediating symbolic distance, but not necessarily a sense of closure, to the past. 'Every Irishman is an actor,' John Ford once remarked. 'The Irish and the coloured people are the most natural actors in the world.'[129] This point is underscored to political effect in *The Rising of the Moon* (1957) when an escaped republican prisoner (Donal Donnelly) twice evades the law through acting and masquerade, first as a nun and then as a ballad-singer, as if bringing theatre into the streets.[130] The association of the Irish with African-American culture suggests that Ford is intent on questioning not only an unthinking adherence to one's own diasporic inheritance, but to the dominant values of the host American culture, and what is required to survive in it.

Sean Thornton's engagement with the moral economy of rural Ireland allows him to break from the impasse of unfettered American individualism, according to which all value is subordinated to private gain, market relations and forms of competition whose ultimate logic is violence. Though Sean Thornton stays in Innisfree with Mary Kate, Ford seemed to bring this deeply critical stance towards dominant American values back with him to the United States. Thus, for example, while it is easy to attribute the violence of Sean's dragging of Mary Kate through the fields to the backwardness of rural Ireland, in *The Searchers*, Martin's (Jeffrey Hunter) appalling treatment of his Indian wife Look (Beulah Archuletta), extending to kicking her down a hill, suggests that it may have as much to do with Sean's American as his Irish background.[131] *The Searchers* may be seen as the most eloquent of a new genre of ethnographic westerns sensitive to the plight of Native Americans, but it is striking that even though John Wayne, in his Ethan role, has thoroughly mastered Comanche mores and customs, he has not brought with him Sean Thornton's cultural sympathy and his willingness to participate in other ways of relating to land, sexuality and violence. The result is a form of racist pathology, in which Ethan's desire to annihilate the savage without is a means of purging the unacknowledged savage within, the forces that connived to produce Sean's killer instinct in the ring.

Ford's life and work may be seen as an attempt to retrieve the American dream by transferring its sympathies from White, European legacies of colonial expansion to the rights of other cultures and indigenous peoples considered to be mere obstacles to progress, and his Irishness was central to this task. Asked by a British journalist, Philip Jenkinson, whether he viewed the systematic destruction of the Indians as a blot on American history, Ford answered gruffly:

> 'My sympathy is all with the Indians. Do you consider the invasion of the Black and Tans in Ireland as a blot on English history . . .?'

'Some historians would,' Jenkinson carefully replied, 'but some historians would regard the systematic destruction of the Indians as something terrible.'

'I'm not talking about the Indians, I'm talking about the Black and Tans,' Ford snapped.

'I don't know enough about it' [Jenkinson replied].

'It's the same thing.'[132]

It is striking that Ford returns to the scene of the crime, the burning of the Thornton home in Spiddal by the Black and Tans which cast a shadow over *The Quiet Man*, to recover his own often displaced sympathies with the Indians. In terms of pacing and formal rhythms, the sense of ritual which punctuates *The Quiet Man* found its way back into the linear narratives of Ford's late westerns, impeding the triumphant march of progress and opening up new critical spaces for the excluded 'Other', most notably in his homage to dispossesed Native Americans, *Cheyenne Autumn* (1960). It is, indeed, the somatic memory of ritual that saves Debbie – and perhaps Ethan from himself – at the end of *The Searchers*, when, holding her high to dash out her brains on the rocks, the gesture triggers off an involuntary memory of his 'homecoming' at the beginning of the film when he lifts the younger Debbie, thinking she is her sister Lucy. 'Let's go home, Debbie' could be the words of a Sean Thornton cast adrift on the desert rather than the rose-gardens of Innisfree. Whatever about *E.T.* and aliens from outer space, Ford's films encourage those who are treated as aliens in this world – the dispossessed, immigrants, migrant workers, Native Americans, African-Americans, the unemployed, whiskey doctors, fallen women, rebels – to renew the search for home this side of paradise.

CREDITS

Title:	The Quiet Man
Director:	John Ford
Release Year:	1952
Production Company:	Republic Pictures
Corporation	
Country:	USA

Cast:

John Wayne	Sean Thornton
Maureen O'Hara	Mary Kate Danaher
Barry Fitzgerald	Michaeleen Oge Flynn
Ward Bond	Father Lonergan
Victor McLaglen	'Red' Will Danaher
Mildred Natwick	Mrs Tillane
Francis Ford	Dan Tobin
Eileen Crowe	Mrs Playfair
May Craig	Woman at Railway Station
Arthur Shields	Mr Playfair
Charles B. Fitzsimons	Forbes
Jack MacGowran	Feeney

Credits:

John Ford	Director
John Ford	Producer
Merian C. Cooper	Producer
Andrew V. McLaglen	Assistant Director
Frank S. Nugent and Richard Llewellyn	Script
Maurice Walsh	Original story
Winton C. Hoch	Photography
Archie J. Stout	2nd Unit Photographer
Jack Murray	Editor
Frank Hotaling	Art Director
Victor Young	Music

Running time:	130 mins
Field length:	11632 ft or 3547 mtrs.
Colour code:	Colour
Colour system:	Technicolor

Notes

1   Charles Ramirez Berg, 'The Margin as Centre: the Multicultural Dynamics of John Ford's Westerns', in *John Ford Made Westerns: Filming the Legend in the Sound Era*, eds. Gaylyn Studlar and Matthew Bernstein (Bloomington: University of Indiana Press, 2001), p. 76.

2   As Spielberg himself commented on this sequence: 'I've always loved that moment in *The Quiet Man* with the wind blowing and the way he held her by the hand without forcing her, he just allowed her to allow herself to come in for the kiss – well, he kind of forced her, he put her in a half-Nelson actually . . .' This ambivalence towards Sean's treatment of Mary Kate became, as we shall see, a key point of contention in critical responses to the film, and Spielberg is careful to note that the point of showing such fantasies is that 'you can look at them from every single angle, and question them . . .' (Interview on '100 Best Films of the Century', Channel 4, 2001).

3   Martin Scorsese, *Scorsese on Scorsese*, eds. David Thompson and Ian Christie (London: Faber and Faber, 1989), p. 80.

4   In addition to the two Oscars awarded, there were nominations for 'Best Picture', 'Best Supporting Actor' (Victor McLaglen), 'Best Writing, Screenplay' (Frank Nugent), 'Best Art Direction, Set Decoration, Colour' (Frank Hotaling, John McCarthy Jr., Charles S. Thompson), 'Best Sound Recording' (Daniel J. Bloomberg).

5   Lance Pettitt, *Screening Ireland: Film and Television Representation* (Manchester: Manchester University Press, 2000), p. 64.

6   Gerry McNee, *In the Footsteps of* The Quiet Man (Edinburgh: Mainstream Publishing, 1990), p. 9. Unabashedly subscribing to the cult of *The Quiet Man* which it celebrates, McNee's work and Des MacHale's more recent and comprehensive guide, *The Complete Guide to* The Quiet Man (Belfast: Appletree, 1999), are the only book-length accounts of the film to date.

7   'The Best Movies Ever Made: Favorite Flick #44', <http://www.shopping-entertainment-online.com/favorite50/44-the-quiet-man.htm>.

8   Joseph McBride, *Searching for John Ford* (New York: St Martin's Press, 2001), p. 512.

9   See O'Hara's account in McNee, p. 64.

10 John Ford, letter to Lord Killanin, 9 August 1946, Killanin Papers, Library of the Film Institute of Ireland, Dublin.

11 John Ford, letter to Lord Killanin, 20 September 1950, Killanin Papers.

12   Tag Gallagher, *John Ford: the Man and his Films* (Berkeley: University of California Press, 1986), p. 279.

13   MacHale, p. 37.

14   Peter Bogdanovich, *John Ford* (Berkeley: University of California Press, 1978), p. 76.

15   See, for example, Raymond Williams, *The Country and the City* (London: Chatto and Windus, 1973); John Barrell, *The Dark Side of the Landscape: the Rural Poor in English Painting 1730–1840* (Cambridge: Cambridge University Press, 1980); Ann Bermingham, *Landscape and Ideology: the English Rustic Tradition, 1740–1860* (Berkeley: University of California Press, 1986).

16   Barrell, *The Dark Side of the Landscape*, p. 78.

17   For the Irish resonances in 'The Deserted Village', see Declan Kiberd, *Irish Classics* (London: Granta, 2000), Chapter 8. Goldsmith's upbringing at Lissoy, County Westmeath, certainly left its mark on the poem – Goldsmith's sister in a letter identifies the famous village schoolmaster as being from Lissoy – but it is most likely that the imagined rural scenes draw on both an Irish and an English provenance.

18   Barrell, *The Dark Side of the Landscape*, pp. 78–79.

19   McBride, p. 27.

20   For a valuable discussion of Ford's narrative use of ritual in relation to his Catholicism, see Paul Giles, 'The Cinema of Catholicism: John Ford and Robert Altman', in *Unspeakable Images: Ethnicity and the American Cinema*, ed. Lester D. Friedman (Urbana: University of Illinois Press, 1991), pp. 140–166.

21   McNee, p. 89.

22   Berg, p. 76. For a breakdown of Ford's emphasis on the wide-ranging ethnic and immigrant composition of the US Cavalry, including Mexican, Irish-American, German-American, Franco-American, Polish-American, African-American and Native American, see McBride, p. 454.

23   Ford, cited in Joseph Curran, *Hibernian Green on the Silver Screen: the Irish and American Movies* (New York: Greenwood Press, 1989), p. 84.

24   Richard Neupert, *The End: Narration and Closure in the Cinema* (Detroit: Wayne State University Press, 1996), p. 44.

25   See, for example, MacHale, p. 208, and the local objections to the depictions of domestic violence recorded in McNee, p. 100. I discuss this in greater detail in Chapter 3.

26   Brandon French, 'The Joys of Marriage: *The Quiet Man*', in *On the*

Verge of Revolt: Women in American Films of the Fifties (New York: Frederick Ungar, 1978), p. 18.

27   Richard Schickel, 'The Man Who Shot the West', *New York Times Book Review* (9 January 2000), p. 9.

28   Quoted in Vincent Dowling, *Astride the Moon: a Theatrical Life* (Dublin: Wolfhound Press, 2000), p. 345.

29   J. Marshall Robb, quoted in Steve Matheson, *Maurice Walsh, Storyteller* (Dingle: Brandon Books, 1985), p. 37. I am indebted to Matheson's study for the main biographical details of Walsh's life.

30   Maurice Walsh, 'My Fey Lady', in *Son of a Tinker* (1951), p. 167, quoted in Matheson, p. 20.

31   Maurice Walsh, 'Then Came the Captain's Daughter', *The Quiet Man*, Part One (Tralee: Anvil Books, 1964), p. 37. (All subsequent references will be cited in parentheses in the text.) This imprint is the only edition of *Green Rushes* in print, renamed to capitalize on the success of the film.

32   Notwithstanding the romantic sentiments which pervade *Green Rushes*, Walsh's depiction of convivial relations between the officer class and their IRA counterparts was not entirely without foundation. Brigadier-General Lucas, for example, was captured while fishing with fellow officers on the Blackwater and, having escaped from his captors, 'was reported as calling them "delightful people", saying he had been treated as a gentleman by gentlemen'. See Robert Kee, *Ourselves Alone* (London: Quartet, 1976), p. 102.

33   The original *Saturday Evening Post* version is republished in MacHale, pp. 17–26.

34   It is noticeable that – in keeping with the patriarchal ethos of inheritance in the Irish countryside – the male sex of the child is taken as preordained, as is again clear when Paddy Bawn addresses his wife at the end: 'Mother of my son, will you come home with me?' (Walsh, p. 138).

35   Fitzgerald, however, played one of the captured British soldiers in Denis Johnston's fine film adaptation of the Frank O'Connor story *Guests of the Nation* in 1935 and was a regular in O'Casey roles, including that of Fluther in John Ford's *The Plough and the Stars* (1936).

36   Mickeen Oge – as his name indicates – is much younger in the story, and we learn later that he has paid a high price for his patriotism: 'The foolish lad! Six months in jail, five weeks on a hunger strike, a year hiding in the hills; and the spirit is not yet broken in him' (Walsh, p. 151).

37   Joseph McBride and Michael Wilmington, *John Ford* (London: Secker & Warburg, 1974), p. 110.

38   Ernie O'Malley, *On Another Man's Wound* (1936; Tralee: Anvil, 1979).

39   Maureen O'Hara, quoted in Richard English, *Ernie O'Malley: IRA Intellectual* (Oxford: Oxford University Press, 1998), p. 65. O'Malley was subsequently employed in 1956 as 'Technical Director' on Ford's *The Rising of the Moon* (1957), whose final part, '1921', had a more explicit storyline dealing with the Troubles.

40   MacHale, p. 38.

41   Jim Rees and Liam Charlton, *Arklow – Last Stronghold of Sail: Arklow Ships from 1850–1985* (Arklow, 1986), cited in McBride, pp. 139–140.

42   Cited in Dan Ford, *Pappy: the Life of John Ford* (New York: De Capo, 1998), p. 23.

43   See Tim Pat Coogan, *Michael Collins* (London: Arrow, 1990), p. 266.

44   Dan Ford, p. 23, and McBride, p. 141. Though some versions of Ford's experience of the Troubles may be less than reliable, the accuracy of his account of the boat journey calls into question the readiness of some commentators to dismiss his recollections outright as 'a vivid flight of fancy, aimed at a gullible Irish public' (MacHale, p. 38).

45   Information provided by Cormac Ó Comhraí, completing an MA thesis in history at NUI, Galway (2002), on the intelligence aspects of the Irish War of Independence. Ó Comhraí points out that the Black and Tan atrocities extended as far as the burning of Moycullen, the other side of the mountain from Spiddal (I am grateful to Professor Gearóid Ó Tuathaigh for relaying this information). Though Ford actually mentions in his letter that the truce was in force during his visit, in another account of the same incident, fifteen years later, he gives the impression that the burning of the Thornton home took place in December 1921 and that he witnessed old Mr and Mrs Thornton standing on the road in silent anger (letter to Sean O'Casey, 9 March 1936, quoted in McBride, p. 141).

46   'Midnight Burnings', *Freeman's Journal* (17 May 1921). I am grateful to Caoilfhionn Ní Bheacháin for this reference, and to Thomas Byrne for additional assistance on Spiddal local history.

47   Thornton also featured as the RIC Sergeant in '1921', the final instalment of *The Rising of the Moon*.

48   John Ford, letter to Lord Killanin, 25 October 1951, Killanin Papers. As early as *Hangman's House* (1928) Ford addressed the Irish Troubles (as is evident from the almost contemporary British army uniforms and artillery in the film), and they were, of course, central to *The*

Informer (1935), *The Plough and the Stars* (1936), the final episode of *The Rising of the Moon* and, to a lesser extent, *Young Cassidy* (1965).

49   Richard Llewellyn, quoted in Scott Eyman, *Print the Legend: the Life and Times of John Ford* (New York: Simon & Schuster, 1999), pp. 398–399, from the draft notes, Ford Papers, Lilly Library, Indiana University. Though superceded by McBride's monumental biography, Eyman's study and Dan Ford's pioneering biography are the other indispensable works on Ford's life.

50   John Ford, quoted in MacHale, p. 35. Sean Nunan was Irish Minister to the US (1947–1950) under the Inter-Party government of 1948–1951, and was Lord Killanin's contact in the Department of External Affairs. In a letter to Killanin, 30 April 1953, Ford requests him, half in jest, to tell Nunan that he has eye trouble, just like de Valera.

51   Gallagher, p. 284.

52   Frank Nugent, quoted in MacHale, p. 52.

53   Nicholas Dames, 'Austen's Nostalgics', *Representations*, No. 73 (Winter 2001), p. 117.

54   Dames, p. 117.

55   William Falconer, *A Dissertation on the Influence of the Passions upon Disorders of the Body* (London, 1788), pp. 90–91, quoted in Dames, p. 122.

56   Thomas Arnold, *Observations on the Nature, Kinds, Causes, and Prevention of Insanity, Lunacy, or Madness* (Leicester, 1782), p. 266, quoted in Dames, p. 124.

57   Dames, p. 127

58   Dames, pp. 127–128.

59   As the actor Charles Fitzsimons described it: 'When I toasted the couple my line was "May they live in peace and national freedom." But John Ford panicked a bit thinking the word "national" might offend and it leads to a slight break in sound. There was supposed to be a greater IRA – Black and Tans theme but he changed it' (McNee p. 155). That Yates was, in fact, responsible is pointed out by McBride, p. 772.

60   MacHale, p. 171.

61   As Joseph McBride acutely observes, 'this horrific image was echoed in Ford's 1956 Western *The Searchers*, when Ethan Edwards (John Wayne) and Martin Pauley (Jeffrey Hunter) discover their family home burning after an Indian attack. Before the action of *Rio Grande* begins, Wayne's Kirby Yorke has burned his wife's home' (McBride, p. 141). Given that Yorke's wife is played by Maureen O'Hara, and

part of the motivation of the action is the undoing of this primal transgression, *Rio Grande* uncannily foreshadows *The Quiet Man*.

62 When interviewed by Peter Bogdanovich, Ford himself stated that this conspicuous waste of money was one of the few mistakes in the script (Bogdanovich, p. 91). But, as Ed Buscombe points out in relation to the most memorable scenes in *The Searchers*, Ethan Edwards' gesture with his arm, and his walking away, are not in the original script either (*The Searchers* [London: British Film Institute, 2000], p. 75).

63 French, p. 15.

64 For an extensive discussion of emigration and Irish cinema, see Kevin Rockett, 'The Irish Migrant and Film', in *The Creative Migrant, the Irish World Wide: History, Heritage, Identity*, 3, ed. Patrick O'Sullivan (Leicester: Leicester University Press, 1994), pp. 170–191.

65 Maureen Turim, *Flashbacks in Film: Memory and History* (New York: Routledge, 1989), 27ff.

66 Wendy Holden, *Shell-Shock: the Psychological Impact of War* (London: Channel 4/Macmillan, 1998), p. 22.

67 Bela Balazs, *Theory of Film*, trans. Edith Bone (London: Dennis Dobson, 1952), p. 120.

68 See Ralph Rosenblum and Robert Karen, *When the Shooting Stops . . . the Cutting Begins: a Film Editor's Story* (New York: De Capo Press, 1979), 142ff. As the fluidity between terms such as 'cross-cut', 'cut-back', 'switch-back', 'dissolve', etc., suggests, in the 1910–20 period, early uses of flashbacks may have come across to spectators much as 'flash-cuts' did in the late 1950s, given the unfamiliarity with – and often baffled responses to – even more accessible techniques such as parallel editing.

69 Susan J. Brison, 'Trauma Narratives and the Re-Making of the Self', in *Acts of Memory: Cultural Recall in the Present*, eds. Mieke Bal, Jonathan Crewe and Leo Spitzer (Hanover, NH: University Press of North England, 1999), p. 40.

70 I discuss a similar anomalous use of the flashback in relation to the travelogue/documentary *The Spell of Ireland* (1959) in the Conclusion to this book.

71 Neupert, p. 60.

72 Neupert, p. 60.

73 Erwin Panofsky, '*Et in Arcadia Ego*: Poussin and the Elegiac Tradition', in *Meaning in the Visual Arts* (New York: Doubleday, 1955), p. 301.

74   Panofsky, p. 309.

75   Panofsky, p. 317.

76   French, p. 20.

77   In a response to Jean Mitry, cited in McBride, p. 455.

78   See Sean O'Suilleabhain, *Irish Wake Amusements* (Cork: Mercier Press, 1967), 92ff. As one episcopal letter enjoined, directing the clergy to stamp out abuses at wakes: 'They must point out to the parishioners that the playing of lewd games at wakes, where Death should rather be pondered on, is synonymous with turning their backs on the faith. The clergy must take care to ensure that indecent talk and especially the sinful practice of travestying the Sacrament of Marriage are abolished on such occasions' (quoted in O'Suilleabhain, p. 153).

79   See Michael Lowy, *Romanticism Against the Tide of Modernity* (Durham, NC: Duke University Press, 2002).

80   Peter Lehmann, 'How the West Wasn't Won: the Repression of Capitalism in John Ford's Westerns', in Studlar and Bernstein, p. 137.

81   Gallagher, p. 253.

82   Lehmann, p. 145.

83   J. J. Lee, 'Women and the Church Since the Famine', in *Women in Irish Society*, eds. Margaret McCurtain and Donnchadh Ó Corráin (Dublin: Arlen House, 1978), p. 38.

84   Mary Daly, 'The Irish Family Since the Famine: Continuity and Change', *Irish Journal of Feminist Studies*, Vol. 3, No. 2 (Autumn 1999), pp. 9–10.

85   Lee, p. 38; Gearóid Ó Tuathaigh, 'The Role of Women in Ireland under the New English Order', in McCurtain and Ó Corráin, p. 30. The best recent overview of the role of the dowry is Timothy Guinnane, *The Vanishing Irish: Households, Migration, and the Rural Economy in Ireland, 1850–1914* (Princeton: Princeton University Press, 1997).

86   James MacKillop, '*The Quiet Man* Speaks', in *Contemporary Irish Cinema: from* The Quiet Man *to* Dancing at Lughnasa (Syracuse: Syracuse University Press, 1999), p. 175.

87   Virginia Wright Wexman, *Creating the Couple: Love, Marriage and Hollywood Performance* (Princeton: Princeton University Press, 1993), p. 8.

88   McBride and Wilmington, p. 123.

89   McBride and Wilmington, p. 123. Tradition is construed as a burden here, and that is Sean's initial view; my argument, by contrast, is that

113

it is by working *through* tradition that Sean lifts the burden of his American past. McBride and Wilmington later seem to concur with this when they state of the embrace in the graveyard: 'We are not made to feel here that religion and the past are repressive influences: on the contrary, Sean yearns for their security' (p. 123).

90 These locations are enumerated and described in *The Quiet Man* files in the Killanin Papers.

91 Agee, quoted in McBride, p. 455.

92 Gallagher, p. 279.

93 Gallagher, p. 282.

94 Lindsay Anderson, '*The Quiet Man*' [Review], *Sight and Sound*, Vol. 22, No. 1 (July/September 1952), p. 25.

95 One suspects at times that the subjective camera associated with Sean in the film also extended to the experience of the weather on the set. According to Maureen O'Hara, when interviewed on the set, the filming of *The Quiet Man* was accompanied by unusually good weather: 'I've never experienced such luck on any film. When we require brilliant sunshine we get it. As far as I am concerned Ireland is the star of the picture' (McNee, p. 70). Local people's memories back this up, recalling that the summer had been the best for years (McNee, p. 114). By contrast, the cinematographer, Winston Hoch, complained that 'in the six weeks we were in Ireland we had only six days of unbroken sunshine ... I had to light each scene three different ways: for sunshine, for clouds, and for rain. I worked out a set of signals with the gaffer, and we were ready no matter what the light was. But I tell you, it wasn't easy' (quoted in Dan Ford, p. 243).

96 Peter Stowell, *John Ford* (Boston, MA: Twayne, 1986), p. 140.

97 Aidan Pender, 'Hand of Maestro in *The Quiet Man*', *Evening Herald* (17 May 1952), p. 4; Anon., 'An Eye for the US Market', *Irish Independent* (19 May 1952), p. 8.

98 Herbert Yates, quoted in Ronald L. Davis, *John Ford: Hollywood's Old Master* (Newman: University of Oklahoma Press, 1995).

99 Killanin Papers.

100 For this argument, see Ed Buscombe, 'Sound and Colour', in *Movies and Methods*, Vol. II, ed. Bill Nicholls (Berkeley: University of California Press, 1985), pp. 83–91.

101 Gallagher, p. 283.

102 His shadow is, in fact, momentarily cast on the backdrop in the lower left-hand corner, throwing a shadow over the landscape in more ways than one.

103 Stowell, p. 139.

104 Even before this, the first shot of Sean is through the window as he gazes at the countryside from his railway carriage at Castletown station.

105 John McGahern, *That They May Face the Rising Sun* (London: Faber & Faber, 2002), p. 68.

106 Charles Affron, *Cinema and Sentiment* (Chicago: University of Chicago Press, 1982), p. 49.

107 Douglas Sirk, quoted in Fred Camper, 'A Time to Love and a Time to Die', in *Douglas Sirk*, eds. Laura Mulvey and Jon Halliday (Edinburgh: Edinburgh Festival, 1972), p. 87.

108 Gallagher, p. 185.

109 Gallagher, p. 195.

110 See Richard Neupert's insightful breakdown of this sequence, p. 69.

111 MacHale, p. 208.

112 Conrad M. Arensberg and Solon T. Kimball, *Family and Community in Ireland* (Cambridge, MA: Harvard University Press, 1948), p. 137.

113 Ford is carrying over a convention from the early years of cinema that persisted in different forms after the advent of sound, as in his own *The Black Watch* (1929) and the parade towards the camera at the end of *Judge Priest* (1934). On this, see Gallagher, p. 105.

114 For a story to pass effortlessly from a framing voice-over or series of flashbacks to a clear resolution, the narration has to be securely re-established in an authoritative narrative position, that is, in the 'real' world established outside subjective narration (usually shown at the beginning as well, before the framing flashback begins, as in the Vienna of *Letter from an Unknown Woman*, dir. Max Ophuls, 1948). Irresolvable ambiguities arise when, for example, the narrator is killed, as in *Laura* (dir. Otto Preminger, 1946), *Sunset Boulevard* (dir. Billy Wilder, 1950) or *American Beauty* (dir. Sam Mendes, 1999), before the subjective narration has any possibility of re-entering the 'real' world.

115 MacHale, p. 197. See also McBride: 'While it's true that Ford finds great enjoyment in the spectacle of Sean dragging Mary Kate through the fields after she refuses to sleep with him, it's important to understand that this is all a charade concocted by Mary Kate. Like the fight scene that follows, it is not so much a physical battle as a piece of theatre performed to make a point before the community' (p. 515). It is not clear, in fact, that Mary Kate has refused to sleep with Sean, for there is a strong suggestion that their marriage is consummated the night before she leaves for the train (see MacHale, pp. 196–197). This would be consistent with the reading that their

holding out against Red Will is for public consumption, rather than a private impasse between them.

116   French, p. 19.

117   Neupert, p. 66.

118   Giles, p. 143.

119   Stephanie Rains, 'Home From Home: Diasporic Images of Ireland in Film and Television', unpublished paper, 'Defining Colonies' Conference, Galway (June 1999). I am greatly indebted to Stephanie Rains for providing me with a copy of this and a related paper, which are part of an ongoing research project on American cultural perceptions of Ireland.

120   I am grateful to Dr Marion Casey, New York University, who first drew my attention to this travelogue film. See also the discussion in Rains, 'Home From Home'.

121   See, for example, the showcasing of Croagh Patrick in *National Geographic*, April 1981 and September 1994. Considered in this light, Ireland becomes a site of pilgrimage rather than tourism – though it is genealogy and Ireland's cultural riches that are expected to regenerate the soul, rather than religion.

122   The promotional blurb on *The Spell of Ireland* claims that the film 'was produced in Ireland in the 1940s in natural colour . . . It is a trip back to 1940.' If so, it is even more remarkable as an uncanny anticipation of *The Quiet Man*.

123   Donald S. Connery, *The Irish* (London: Eyre & Spottiswoode, 1969), pp. 14, 91. For a related discussion of Connery, see McBride, pp. 514–515.

124   Giles, p. 143.

125   In his exemplary monograph on *The Searchers* ((London: British Film Institute, 2000), Ed Buscombe discusses Stuart Byron's analysis of eleven major films that show the direct influences of the film, but even this fails to account for its substantial reworking of the centrality of captivity narratives in American culture. See Buscombe, *The Searchers*, pp. 68–9, citing Stuart Byron, ' *The Searchers*: Cult Movie of the New Hollywood', *New York Magazine* (5 March 1979).

126   In addition to the films discussed below, Eugene Brady's *The Nephew* (1998) transforms the visiting Irish-American relative into a hip African-American, whose journey to Ireland also unlocks the traumatic secrets of his mother's past. The potential for opening up the kind of cross-cultural interactions suggested by Ford's treatment of ethnicity is not fully explored in the film, however. In the comedy *The Matchmaker* (dir. Mark Joffe, 1997), an Irish-American politician sends

his assistant to Ireland to trace his Irish genealogy in order to boost his Irish-American vote in Boston, only to reveal in the end that he is of Hungarian ancestry. (For insightful discussions of both films, see Stephanie Rains, 'Memory and History: the Irish-American Genealogy Industry', unpublished paper, 'Diasporic Communications' Conference, University of Westminster, September 2001.) In Neil Jordan's *The Miracle* (1991), the returned visitor is the enigmatic mother of the young protagonist of the film, who uses the alibi of performing in a musical version of 'Destry Rides Again' in Dublin to return home, both Oedipally and geographically. Jordan's earlier comic farce, *High Spirits* (1988), deals with the visit of an Irish-American package tour to a spoof haunted castle in Ireland which turns out to house 'real' ghosts. The returned American in *The Lonely Passion of Judith Hearne* (dir. Jack Clayton, 1987) operates outside the ambit of *The Quiet Man* but, as a counterpoint to its happy ending, illuminates the destructive consequences of an unsuccessful Irish-American romance. For a whimsical version of a successful romance between an American journalist and an Irish colleen, complete with leprechaun, which pre-dates *The Quiet Man*, see *The Luck of the Irish* (dir. Henry Koster, 1948).

127 Martin McLoone, *Irish Film: the Emergence of a Contemporary Cinema* (London: British Film Institute, 2001), p. 194.

128 Jane M. Shattuc, *The Talking Cure: TV Talk Shows and Women* (New York: Routledge, 1997), pp. 120–121.

129 John Ford, quoted in Gallagher, p. 279.

130 This is a recurring device in Ford's films; e.g. Citizen Hogan, the Irish rebel in *Hangman's House* who returns from the French Foreign Legion to bring the killer of his sister, D'arcy, to justice, disguises himself as a mendicant friar, with suitable hood; and, of course, the whole community disguise themselves as Protestants at the end of *The Quiet Man*.

131 As Tag Gallagher notes, Ford takes great care to frame such scenes within distancing flashbacks, or stories within stories, to expose them to critical scrutiny rather than endorsing them (pp. 326).

132 John Ford and Philip Jenkinson, as recounted in McBride, p. 143. Notwithstanding his turn to the political right during the Vietnam war, Ford could still write in 1967 to Lord Killanin that he saw *Cheyenne Autumn* (1964) as telling 'the Indian side of the story. This, I think, will be a welcome relief to the movies and TVs of the past' (letter to Lord Killanin, 30 July 1967, Killanin Papers).

Bibliography

Affron, Charles. *Cinema and Sentiment*. Chicago: University of Chicago Press, 1982.

Anderson, Lindsay. '*The Quiet Man*' [Review]. *Sight and Sound*, Vol. 22, No. 1 (July/September 1952).

Anon. 'An Eye for the US Market'. *Irish Independent* (19 May 1952).

Arensberg, Conrad M., and Solon T. Kimball. *Family and Community in Ireland*. Cambridge, MA: Harvard University Press, 1948.

Balazs, Bela. *Theory of Film*, trans. Edith Bone. London: Dennis Dobson, 1952.

Barrell, John. *The Dark Side of the Landscape: the Rural Poor in English Painting 1730–1840*. Cambridge: Cambridge University Press, 1980.

Berg, Charles Ramirez. 'The Margin as Centre: the Multicultural Dynamics of John Ford's Westerns', *John Ford Made Westerns: Filming the Legend in the Sound Era*. Eds. Gaylyn Studlar and Matthew Bernstein. Bloomington: University of Indiana Press, 2001, pp. 75–101.

Bermingham, Ann. *Landscape and Ideology: the English Rustic Tradition, 1740–1860*. Berkeley: University of California Press, 1986.

Bogdanovich, Peter. *John Ford*. Berkeley: University of California Press, 1978.

Brison, Susan J. 'Trauma Narratives and the Re-Making of the Self'. *Acts of Memory: Cultural Recall in the Present*. Eds. Mieke Bal, Jonathan Crewe and Leo Spitzer. Hanover, NH: University Press of North England, 1999, pp. 39–54.

Buscombe, Ed. *The Searchers*. London: British Film Institute, 2000.

—— 'Sound and Colour'. *Movies and Methods*, Vol. II. Ed. Bill Nicholls. Berkeley: University of California Press, 1985, pp. 83–91.

Byrne, Des. *The Quiet Man Quiz Book 1000*. An Chéad Chló: Chló Iar-Chonnachta Teo., 1992. Daly: pp. 1–21.

Byron, Stuart. '*The Searchers*: Cult Movie of the New Hollywood'. *New York Magazine* (5 March 1979).

Camper, Fred. 'A Time to Love and a Time to Die'. *Douglas Sirk*. Eds. Laura Mulvey and Jon Halliday. Edinburgh: Edinburgh Festival, 1972. 79–88.

Connery, Donald S. *The Irish*. London: Eyre & Spottiswoode, 1969.

Coogan, Tim Pat. *Michael Collins*. London: Arrow, 1990.

Curran, Joseph. *Hibernian Green on the Silver Screen: the Irish and American Movies*. New York: Greenwood Press, 1989.

Daly, Mary. 'The Irish Family Since the Famine: Continuity and Change'. *Irish Journal of Feminist Studies*, Vol. 3, No. 2 (Autumn 1999), pp. 1–21.

Dames, Nicholas. 'Austen's Nostalgics'. *Representations*, No. 73 (Winter 2001), pp. 117–143.

Davis, Ronald L. *John Ford: Hollywood's Old Master*. Newman: University of Oklahoma Press, 1995.

Dowling, Vincent. *Astride the Moon: a Theatrical Life*. Dublin: Wolfhound Press, 2000.

English, Richard. *Ernie O'Malley: IRA Intellectual*. Oxford: Oxford University Press, 1998.

Eyman, Scott. *Print the Legend: the Life and Times of John Ford*. New York: Simon & Schuster, 1999.

Ford, Dan. *Pappy: the Life of John Ford*. New York: De Capo, 1998.

French, Brandon. 'The Joys of Marriage: *The Quiet Man*'. *On the Verge of Revolt: Women in American Films of the Fifties*. New York: Frederick Ungar, 1978, pp. 13–22.

Gallagher, Tag. *John Ford: the Man and His Films*. Berkeley: University of California Press, 1986.

Gibbons, Luke. *Transformations in Irish Culture*. Cork: Cork University Press, 1996.

Giles, Paul. 'The Cinema of Catholicism: John Ford and Robert Altman', *Unspeakable Images: Ethnicity and the American Cinema*, Ed. Lester D. Friedman. Urbana: University of Illinois Press, 1991. 140–166.

Guinnane, Timothy. *The Vanishing Irish: Households, Migration, and the Rural Economy in Ireland, 1850–1914*. Princeton: Princeton University Press, 1997.

Holden, Wendy. *Shell-Shock: the Psychological Impact of War*. London: Channel 4/Macmillan, 1998.

Kee, Robert. *Ourselves Alone*. London: Quartet, 1976.

Kiberd, Declan. *Irish Classics*. London: Granta, 2000.

Killanin, Lord. Killanin Papers, Library of the Film Institute of Ireland, Dublin.

Lee, J. J. 'Women and the Church since the Famine'. *Women in Irish Society*. Eds. Margaret McCurtain and Donnchadh Ó Corráin. Dublin: Arlen House, 1978, pp. 37–45.

Lehmann, Peter. 'How the West Wasn't Won: the Repression of Capitalism in John Ford's Westerns'. *John Ford Made Westerns*. Eds. Gaylyn Studlar and Matthew Bernstein. Bloomington: Indiana University Press, 2001. 132–153.

Lowy, Michael. *Romanticism against the Tide of Modernity*. Durham, NC: Duke University Press, 2002.

McBride, Joseph. *Searching for John Ford*. New York: St Martin's Press, 2001.

119

McBride, Joseph, and Michael Wilmington. *John Ford*. London: Secker & Warburg, 1974.

McGahern, John. *That They May Face the Rising Sun*. London: Faber & Faber, 2002), p. 68.

MacHale, Des. *The Complete Guide to* The Quiet Man. Belfast: Appletree, 1999.

MacKillop, James, '*The Quiet Man* Speaks'. *Contemporary Irish Cinema: From* The Quiet Man *to* Dancing at Lunaghasa. Ed. James MacKillop. Syracuse: Syracuse University Press, 1999, pp. 169–181.

McLoone, Martin. *Irish Film: the Emergence of a Contemporary Cinema*. London: British Film Institute, 2001.

McNee, Gerry. *In the Footsteps of* The Quiet Man. Edinburgh: Mainstream Publishing, 1990.

Matheson, Steve. *Maurice Walsh, Storyteller*. Dingle: Brandon Books, 1985.

Neupert, Richard. *The End: Narration and Closure in the Cinema*. Detroit: Wayne State University Press, 1996.

O'Malley, Ernie. *On Another Man's Wound*. 1936; Tralee: Anvil, 1979.

O'Suilleabhain, Sean. *Irish Wake Amusements*. Cork: Mercier Press, 1967.

Ó Tuathaigh, Gearóid. 'The Role of Women in Ireland under the New English Order'. *Women in Irish Society*. Eds. Margaret McCurtain and Donnchadh Ó Corráin. Dublin: Arlen House, 1978, pp. 26–36.

Panofsky, Erwin. '*Et in Arcadia Ego*: Poussin and the Elegiac Tradition'. *Meaning in the Visual Arts*. New York: Doubleday, 1955. 295–320.

Pender, Aidan. 'Hand of Maestro in *The Quiet Man*'. *Evening Herald* (17 May 1952).

Pettitt, Lance. *Screening Ireland*. Manchester: Manchester University Press, 2000.

Rains, Stephanie. 'Home From Home: Diasporic Images of Ireland in Film and Television'. Unpublished paper. 'Defining Colonies' Conference, Galway (June 1999).

——. 'Memory and History: the Irish-American Genealogy Industry'. Unpublished paper. 'Diasporic Communications' Conference, University of Westminister (September 2001).

Rockett, Kevin. 'The Irish Migrant and Film'. In *The Creative Migrant, The Irish World Wide: History, Heritage, Identity*, 3. Ed. Patrick O'Sullivan. Leicester: Leicester University Press, 1994, pp. 170–191.

—— Luke Gibbons and John Hill. *Cinema and Ireland*. London: Routledge, 1988.

Rosenblum, Ralph, and Robert Karen. *When the Shooting Stops . . . the Cutting Begins: a Film Editor's Story*. New York: De Capo Press, 1979.

Schickel, Richard. 'The Man Who Shot the West'. *New York Times Book Review* (9 January 2000).

Scorsese, Martin. *Scorsese on Scorsese*. Eds. David Thompson and Ian Christie. London: Faber & Faber, 1989.

Shattuc, Jane M. *The Talking Cure: TV Talk Shows and Women*. New York: Routledge, 1997.

Spielberg, Steven. Interview on '100 Best Films of the Century'. Channel 4 (December 2001).

Stowell, Peter. *John Ford*. Boston: Twayne, 1986.

Turim, Maureen. *Flashbacks in Film: Memory and History*. New York: Routledge, 1989.

Walsh, Maurice. *Blackcock's Feather*. Edinburgh: Chambers, 1980.

——. *Green Rushes*. New York: Fredrerick A. Stokes, 1935.

——. *Son of a Tinker*. London: W. & R. Chambers, 1951.

——. *The Key Above the Door*. 1926; Dublin: Wolfhound Press, 1996.

——. 'The Quiet Man', *Saturday Evening Post* (11 February 1933). Reprinted in MacHale. 17–26.

——. *The Quiet Man*. Tralee: Anvil Books, 1964.

Wexman, Virginia Wright. *Creating the Couple: Love, Marriage and Hollywood Performance*. Princeton: Princeton University Press, 1993.

Williams, Raymond. *The Country and the City*. London: Chatto & Windus, 1973.